A Word in Season

A Word in Season

John Bishop

ABINGDON
NASHVILLE

A WORD IN SEASON

Copyright © 1979 by Abingdon

All rights reserved.
No part of this book may be reproduced in any manner whatsoever without written permission of the publisher except brief quotations embodied in critical articles or reviews. For information address Abingdon, Nashville, Tennessee.

Library of Congress Cataloging in Publication Data

BISHOP, JOHN, 1908-
   A word in season.
     1. Church year sermons. 2. Sermons, American. 3. Methodist Church—Sermons. I. Title.
BV30.B53   252'.6   79-958

ISBN 0-687-46129-4

Scripture quotations noted RSV are from the Revised Standard Version Common Bible, copyrighted © 1973 by the Division of Christian Education of the National Council of the Churches of Christ in the U.S.A.

Chapter 3, "Gifts from Heaven" appeared first in *Church Management: The Clergy Journal*, October 1975, and is reprinted here by permission.

MANUFACTURED BY THE PARTHENON PRESS AT
NASHVILLE, TENNESSEE, UNITED STATES OF AMERICA

To my wife
My constant and loving companion in all seasons

PREFACE

It has long been my contention that in worship and preaching nothing is of more value than following the drama of our redemption by the observance of the Christian Year, a practice which meets with an abundant reward in the appreciation of the congregation. The ordered calendar of the church year is the means of providing a planned program of preaching which will adequately treat the major events and themes of the faith for the worshiping community. To observe times and seasons in spiritual matters may be just as wholesome as observing them in matters of food and drink.

Phillips Brooks once said, "The Christian Year preserves the personality of religion." Observance of the Christian festivals has an ecumenical value. It asserts our essential unity in Christ. The great landmarks of the Christian Year suggest our basic themes for preaching. They compel us to keep close to the fundamental doctrines of the faith. They ensure that in our preaching we constantly return to those mighty acts of God which the church exists to proclaim, as Dr. James Stewart reminds us in his book *Heralds of God*. He says, "The true meaning of Christmas can unfold itself only to those who have climbed the slopes of Advent, the joy of Easter in all its splendor of victory can lay hold only on those who have watched through Lent and have been with Christ in His passion, and the power of Pentecost can be fully revealed only to those who, with one accord in one place, have waited expectantly for the gift from heaven."

The use of the Christian Year does something to save ministers from the perilous subjectivism which expresses itself in the oft-repeated question, "What shall I preach about next Sunday?" Instead of living from hand to mouth the minister can plan his pulpit work so as to secure continuity. Instead of dwelling on marginal themes which are on the fringe of revelation he can deal with the great central truths of the faith.

Matthew Arnold pointed out that the great days of the Christian Year are all historical anniversaries which commemorate the days of the Son of Man either in his earthly or in his exalted life. The Christian Year emphasizes the whole gospel. It covers the full sweep of Christian doctrine. It cultivates the historic sense reminding us that Christianity is a historical religion. It encourages the minister to preach from the Bible and his hearers to read it. It compels him to remember certain biblical themes which he might overlook. It enables him to make an annual journey through the life of Jesus from its foreshadowings in the Old Testament, through the Incarnation to the climax in the Passion and Resurrection, and then to the outcome of that life in the birth of the church at Pentecost.

It is my hope and prayer that these sermons may not only be of assistance to ministers who find it difficult year after year to discover something fresh to say on these days of the Son of Man but may also be a means of informing the minds and strengthening the faith of church members.

CONTENTS

I	Advent—*Waiting for God*...	11
II	Christmas—*Cinderella in the Bible*...........................	19
III	Epiphany—*Gifts from Heaven*..................................	26
IV	Ash Wednesday—*Is Repentance Out of Date?*.........	32
V	First Sunday in Lent—*The Snare of the Shortcut*....	39
VI	Passion Sunday—*Why Is God Silent?*......................	46
VII	Palm Sunday—*The Colt That Carried a King*.........	53
VIII	Maundy Thursday—*The Upper Room*......................	60
IX	Good Friday—*The Cross and the Garden*................	67
X	Easter Day—*The Gospel of the Resurrection*............	73
XI	Ascension Day—*Our Man in Heaven*......................	81
XII	Pentecost—*Three Responses to Pentecost*.................	88
XIII	Trinity Sunday—*God Speaks in Many Voices*..........	95
XIV	All Saints' Day—*The Communion of Saints*............	103

ADVENT

I

Waiting for God

And now, Lord, what wait I for? My hope is in thee. Psalm 39:7
And it shall be said in that day, Lo, this is our God; we have waited for him, we will be glad and rejoice in his salvation.

Isaiah 25:9

To be kept waiting is not an experience which most of us find very pleasant, but it frequently occurs in the common round of daily life. Many times we are held up in some job of work by a trivial detail, and we chafe at the delay and become irritable. We wait for a bus or a train or a plane. Or we have to visit the doctor or the dentist. What a depressing place the waiting room often is. People have always had to live waiting for something—peace or daylight, or husbands to come home or children to get well. People stand in line most of their lives, waiting for a friend or a break or payday or death. It is a strange fact about life in general that, for all our speed, we still have to wait, and because of the speed of modern life we find the waiting frustrating. Our patience wears thin quickly. The waiting game is a difficult game to play, and few of us can claim any skill at it. Jacob's character was far from admirable, but for one quality at least we must give him credit. He was prepared to work and to wait fourteen years to win the woman of his choice.

Think how much we read in the Bible about waiting. The whole book is dominated by the atmosphere of expectation. In the Old Testament the Hebrew people are waiting for the promised Messiah who shall deliver them from the yoke of oppression. In one of the most ancient fragments of their literature it is written: "I have waited for thy salvation, O Lord" (Genesis 49:18). When the prophets came, the habit of a holy expectation was deepened and confirmed. "The Lord is a God of judgment," said Isaiah; "blessed are all they that wait for him" (30:18). The unknown prophet of the exile says: "Thus saith the Lord God, . . . they shall not be ashamed that wait for me" (Isaiah 49:23). The prophets were possessed by a conviction which many of us have lost today. It is the conviction that God is at work in history. The history of men and nations was, to the prophets, the sphere of God's activity.

The Bible is very honest about the times when God does not seem to be around at all, when everything would seem to indicate that he has gone off stage and returned to his own place. Jeremiah bluntly asks God, "Why shouldest thou be as a stranger in the land, and a wayfaring man that turneth aside to tarry for a night?" (14:8). Isaiah cries, "Verily thou art a God that hidest thyself" (45:15). Habakkuk asks, "O Lord, how long shall I cry and thou wilt not hear!" (1:2) The faith of the prophets is a stalwart faith that refuses to die, though men keep asking, "Where is now thy God?" The only thing the Bible has to offer is this word "wait." This is a disturbing word because more often than not it does not seem to get us anywhere. Nothing seems to come of it. In the sad days after the exile, the Jews turned their waiting into a song on their pilgrimage to the temple. "I wait for the Lord, my soul doth wait. . . . My soul waiteth for the Lord more than they that watch for the morning"

WAITING FOR GOD

(Psalm 130:5-6). But when the morning came, it did not look much like the Lord. Through the centuries that followed, the only thing that happened was that wave after wave of conquest swept over the land.

It was among those who were waiting for the consolation of Israel, looking for the long-expected Messiah, like the aged Simeon and Anna, that Christ found his readiest followers. When Jesus called his church into existence, the first lesson that this new Israel had to learn was to wait. He commanded the disciples not to depart from Jerusalem but to wait for the promise of the Father, the gift of the Holy Spirit (Luke 24:49).

Soon the lesson took another form, which to this day we are trying to learn, the form that James gave it when he said: "Be patient . . . unto the coming of the Lord. Behold, the husbandman waiteth for the precious fruit of the earth, and hath long patience for it, until he receive the early and latter rain. Be ye also patient; stablish your hearts: for the coming of the Lord draweth nigh" (5:7-8). The expectation of the coming dominated the mind of the early church. The Bible ends on this note: "Even so, come, Lord Jesus" (Revelation 22:20). Still the world is waiting.

Do you remember Samuel Beckett's play, *Waiting for Godot?* Two disheveled tramps spend their aimless time waiting for Godot. They wait for him because they expect him to explain and bring to an end their insignificance. Every day a child comes to them and informs them that Godot will not arrive until tomorrow. But he never comes at all.

Every human being waits for God. God alone, he believes, can give his life meaning. Man can only fully explain his life in terms of God. Look at the thirty-ninth Psalm. Its theme is the shortness of life. "Lord, make me to know mine end, and the measure of my days, what it is; that I may know how frail I am. Behold, thou hast made my days as an handbreadth; and mine age is as nothing before thee: verily every man at his best state is altogether vanity." Life is a dream which is soon over. So the Psalmist puts the question that troubles every thinking person. What is the meaning of life? What are we looking for? He finds no solution but he does cry out, "My hope is in thee."

Turn now to the eighth chapter of Romans where Paul says: "I reckon that the sufferings of this present time are not worthy to be compared with the glory which shall be revealed in us. For the earnest expectation of the creature waiteth for the manifestation of the sons of God." Paul imagines the whole creation waiting for something with eager longing, waiting for redemption, the redemption of nature, of man, or man's social life. Only as sons of God can we master the world we live in and overcome the ills of life. The waiting Paul speaks of as a prelude to the salvation of the world is waiting for a revelation of a different kind of people, the sons of God. Salvation is to come from men of love and brotherhood. The kingdom of God is not merely something which springs up out of the earth in response to the toil of man, but something which comes down out of heaven from God, for which we must wait.

We live in an age when people must always be doing something, an age which believes in action. We find it hard to believe that time spent in waiting is not wasted time. But waiting is not the opposite of doing. It is the motive for action. It does not disengage us from history. It thrusts us into history, which is still the story God is writing out. Waiting looks to a future that it then helps to bring forth. God has much to give us, but our hands are too full to receive it. That is what waiting means—emptying our hands and making room for God. Dietrich Bonhoeffer in his early days as a minister in Barcelona said this in a sermon on August 12, 1928: "Waiting is an art which our impatient days have forgotten. We expect to pick the ripe fruit when we have only just planted the sapling. . . . The man who does not know the austere pleasure of waiting will never discover the perfect blessing of fulfillment."

The laws of harvest say wait. The discipline of the divine love says wait. Many a word of God says wait. The work is God's. The harvest is his. The future is his. The times and seasons are in his hands. The church must learn to wait, not in the laziness of inactivity but in the obedience of service: not in the gloom of despair but in the patience of hope.

In Bunyan's *Pilgrim's Progress* Christian was taken into a room in the Interpreter's House where sat two little children, each in his chair. The name of the elder was Passion, the name of the younger was Patience. Passion seemed to be much discontented, but Patience was very quiet. Then Christian asked his guide, "What is the reason of the discontent of Passion?" The Interpreter answered: "The governor of them would have him stay for his best things until the beginning of next year but he will have all now but Patience is willing to wait."

There are many people to whom God has given not the joy of working or the task of fighting but the discipline of waiting. This is no new experience. It is as old as the education of mankind. Abraham had long to wait before the child of promise was born. Moses had long to wait, and that in the wilderness, before he became a leader of men. Job had long to wait before God gave him his reward. "Ye have heard of the patience of Job" (James 5:11). Think of our Lord himself. His heart was ablaze with a passion to serve the suffering human race, and he was kept waiting thirty years in the narrow lanes of Nazareth and at a carpenter's bench. When at last his hour was come and he went forth on his mission and drew great crowds by his preaching, it was only to see them, as the days went by, dwindling steadily away. His own family misunderstood him, his best friends forsook him, and then the shadow of death at the last. Yet he laid down his life undaunted and serene because he was quite sure that someday, in God's own time, all his dreams would come true. "And the Lord direct your hearts into . . . the patient waiting for Christ" (II Thessalonians 3:5). If only these fretful hearts of ours could learn from Jesus how to wait. "In your patience," he says, "possess your souls."

The greatest names in history are those who have learned to wait and to wait on the Lord. William Wilberforce learned on his deathbed of the emancipation of the slaves for which he had worked so long and so hard. Someone writing of William Burns, a Presbyterian missionary to China, said, "We must run." It was always William Burns' word until in China God taught him a second lesson, "We must wait." Then his education was finished. Mary Slessor, a Scottish missionary to Africa, once wrote in a letter to a friend, "One test of a really good missionary is this silent, waiting, seemingly useless time. It is difficult to wait. But one text keeps repeating itself to me—'Learn of me.' Christ was never in a hurry. There was no rushing forward, no fretting over what might be. Every day's duties were done as every day brought them, and the rest was left with God."

Waiting—waiting for consolation, waiting for light, waiting for peace, waiting for the harvest, waiting for the kingdom, waiting for larger opportunity and fuller life—that is how God trains us in the grace of patience. One day when Luther was ill, they brought him proof-sheets. "God has touched me sorely," he said; "I have been impatient, but God knows better than I do whereto it serves. Our Lord God is like a printer who sets the letters backward so that here we cannot read them. When we are printed off we shall read all clearly. Meanwhile, we must have patience."

The Advent season calls us to a mood of hope and expectancy. Our part is to wait for God. This is not a method of doing nothing: it is a way of doing everything. It is an attitude of mind and heart. It is the consciousness of our utter dependence on God for the power to do his will, so that at the center of all our activity there is a place of rest and peace. "And it shall be said in that day, Lo, this is our God; we have waited for him, we will be glad and rejoice in his salvation" (Isaiah 25:9 RSV). It means the attitude of expectation. We must be alert for opportunity, as Jesus taught us. The five foolish bridesmaids in the parable waited like the five wise bridesmaids. Their folly was that they let their lamps go out. They were not ready for the big moment for which they had come. So it was at the first coming of the Lord. Many of the people of that day were not expecting God to come in so lowly a form. They were not spiritually alert.

Advent Sunday might be called the festival of the expectant church, for the thoughts which it inspires link together the beginning and the end of the New Testament with this one dominant idea—expectation. We have brought before our minds on Advent Sunday first the Jewish church looking for the promised coming of the Christ. The opening pages of the Gospels present us with a group of faithful souls waiting with eager hearts for the redemption of Israel. In the last pages of the New Testament the book of Revelation presents us once more with groups of faithful people filled with expectation: the same church, now become Christian, waiting for the day when he who came once in great humility shall come again in power and glory. We live between the two comings of Christ. His first coming marks our death to sin; his second coming marks our birth into his eternal kingdom.

The landing of the Allied armies on the beaches of Normandy marked the beginning of the end of World War II. V-Day did not come for many months, but D-Day decided the issue. Christ's D-Day happened in the events of Good Friday and Easter when he launched his final offensive against those forces of evil which proved too strong for the unaided strength of men. His V-Day is coming. He has promised it and proved his promise by the presence of the Holy Spirit through whom even now we share his victory. The battles against evil continue, but whatever their outcome, the war itself has been won and the ultimate issue decided. In that faith we Christians continue the struggle, knowing that Christ has come, Christ is come, and Christ will come again. What he once began he will complete. All these tenses, past, present, and future, must be used if we are to lay hold of the whole truth of Advent. The World Council of Churches climaxed its second assembly at Evanston with this word: "We do not know *what* is coming but we do know *who* is coming. It is he who meets us every day, and will meet us at the end, Jesus Christ our Lord. Therefore we say to you, rejoice in hope."

CHRISTMAS

II

Cinderella in the Bible

You know the grace of our Lord Jesus Christ, that, though he was rich, yet for your sake he became poor, so that by his poverty you might be rich.

II Corinthians 8:9 RSV

The most wonderful and gladdening fact under heaven is that God has given himself to us in his son. God really has entered into humanity, shared it with us, and redeemed it for us. It is the Incarnation that makes Christmas, nothing less. In these words of the apostle Paul we have a summary of the Christmas message, the doctrine of our Lord's incarnation in its briefest, simplest form. "He was rich . . . He became poor . . . for your sakes."

1. "He was rich." Our best commentary here is the well-known passage in the Epistle to the Philippians: "Have this mind among yourselves, which is yours in Christ Jesus, who, though he was in the form of God, did not count equality with God a thing to be grasped, but emptied himself, taking the form of a servant" (2:5-7 RSV). The truth that is taught in these words is that of the preexistence of Jesus: that is to say, Jesus did not begin to be when he was born in Bethlehem. His three and thirty years on earth were but a brief interlude between two eternities. On the eve of his Passion Jesus prayed: "And now, Father, glorify thou

me in thy own presence with the glory which I had with thee before the world was made" (John 17:5 RSV).

Unless the child in his manger-bed is the Eternal Son who before all worlds is one with the Father, then all our Christmas carols and rejoicings are worse than sentiment; they are a gigantic illusion, and the joy and peace in Christian hearts through nineteen centuries has been a pathetic mistake. We believe that God, who through the ages has provoked the spirit of man in dreams, rebuked him by his prophets, uplifted him by the songs of his psalmists, has, at one point in history and at one place on earth, thrust forth his saving arm.

The silence of eternity has been broken up into syllables of human speech: the substance of man's dreams has been given to him in a form that he can clasp. If there were no Christmas, our idea of God might be august and awful: it could never be homely and happy. A God who revealed himself only in suns and systems would remain remote: he could never be intimately near. There is a revelation of God in Nature, but Nature conceals as much as she reveals. I have read of a traveler in Finland who spent a day in the midst of sublime scenery—mountains, cataracts, and mighty forests—but returned home strangely unhappy. In the living room of the house where he was staying were three canaries in a cage. When he entered they became restless, chirping loudly and flitting from perch to perch. Presently he went over and spoke to them, and they became quiet and contented. In that room also was a small dog whining, but when the traveler sat down he came and pawed at his knee and there was a look on his face that said, "Are you never going to notice me?" The man spoke to the dog and patted him, and he too was content. "Then," says the writer, "I knew why all that day I myself had been restless. I had felt God in Nature, but I wanted something more. I wanted to be noticed. I wanted a word, a touch."

That is what the Incarnation means. The glory of God comes into our human nature and speaks to us with an intimacy which it is not within the power of sea or sky or mountain to convey. In Jesus Christ, God is made clear and concrete. He is made available, so that I can grasp him when I fall, bow before him when I want to adore, kneel to him when I want to pray, live in communion with him, and die in his firm embrace.

2. "He became poor." Equal with God he emptied himself. He became so poor that the poorest on earth was richer than one who had not where to lay his head. The world was his: he came unto his own. But he laid aside the glory which he had with the Father and exchanged it for earthly privation and weakness.

Think of the manner of his life from Bethlehem to Calvary. What mother does not remember the loving thought and care which made ready for the coming of her firstborn child? But Mary's son was born in a barn and cradled in a manger. The poets and the artists have transfigured the lowly scene for us, but the reality was far different from their imaginings of it. As was the Savior's birth, so also was his life. There were at least seven children in the home at Nazareth and if, as seems probable, Joseph died early, hard work and much planning would be needed to keep want from the door. And in after years Jesus was still poor. His long journeys were taken on foot. When, by the Sea of Tiberias, he bade his hungry disciples come and break their fast, bread and fish were all he had to set before them. If he ate at a feast it was in another man's house. Women ministered to him of their substance. He had no home of his own. When at last he lay down in the sleep of death it was in the tomb of another they buried him. He was amongst us as one who possessed all things and yet had nothing. This impoverishment was all his own choice. No other hand stripped him of the glory which he had with the Father. "He laid his glory by, He wrapped him in our clay." He was rich; yet by his own act and will he became poor.

He laid aside his omnipotence. Creator of all, he became like one of his creatures. "In all things it behoved him to be made like unto his brethren" (Hebrews 2:17). He laid aside his omniscience and took on the limitations of human knowledge. He grew in knowledge and in favor with God and man. He laid aside his immortality and tasted death for every man, giving his life a ransom for many. I cannot explain how Jesus laid everything aside and emptied himself of all but love. It is a mystery, part of the hidden counsels of God. But this I know, that there was no other way of achieving the desire of his heart.

A modern scholar has shown how all through the Bible there is a Cinderella theme in the long story of God's way with man. Again and again it is the lowly and despised, the unlikely and insignificant people from whom light and salvation came, and in the Christmas story this theme reaches its climax. Let me illustrate this Cinderella motif in the Bible story.

A lonely wronged, forgotten youth lies a prisoner in one of the dungeons of Egypt, a Hebrew named Joseph. And suddenly you read that Pharaoh himself sends and calls him. They bring him hastily out of the dungeon, and Joseph shaves himself and changes his clothes and comes in unto Pharaoh. He is the one person in all the world who has the secret and can interpret Pharaoh's dreams.

A little, nameless servant girl is washing the dishes in the scullery of the great house of Naaman, and she says to her

CINDERELLA IN THE BIBLE

mistress, "Would God my lord were with the prophet that is in Samaria! for he would recover him of his leprosy." And someone tells Naaman what the maid had said, with the result that he goes to Elisha and is healed. Thus the word of the captive Hebrew maid saved the life and health of her master.

A tyrant has a dream. He wakes to find that he cannot recall it. He demands his counselors to tell him the dream. They are quite unable to do so and are in fear of losing their heads, when the chief executioner comes to the king and says, "I have found a man: it is one of the exiles of Judah." It is Daniel, the despised Jew, who saves the situation and declares the dream and gives its interpretation.

A crowd is hungry and there is nothing to set before them. Nothing? Well, there is a lad with five barley loaves and two small fishes, but what are they among so many? It was just then and not before that Jesus said, "Make the crowd sit down."

Now come to the story of Christmas and see how this Cinderella theme in the story of God's way with men comes to its climax. The story begins with shepherds—real men, not as the painters and poets have idealized them, but rough, uncultivated, and boorish. Jewish society classed them with publicans and heathen and despised them as outcasts. But the angels came to the shepherds as they kept watch over their flocks by night. G. K. Chesterton has said that there are some things too important to be entrusted to the educated classes. Perhaps the music of the angels' song is one of those things. At any rate it was not the wise men but the simple shepherds who first heard the sweetest song that this world has ever heard. God humbled himself in the amazing lowliness of the Incarnation. Only the very lowly, the holy and humble of heart, were able to receive him.

Only they had ears attuned to the music of the heavenly host, praising God and saying, "Glory to God in the highest and on earth peace." It was to servants, not masters, to poor, not rich, to unlearned and ignorant men, not to the noble and wise, that the angels came.

3. "For your sake." We know the meaning of the self-emptying of God. It meant a laying aside of glory, a voluntary restraint of power, acceptance of hardship, isolation, ill-treatment, malice, and misunderstanding, ending with a death that involved such spiritual and physical agony that his mind nearly broke under the prospect of it. The manger-cradle, the cruel pinch of poverty, the poisoned hate of foes, the agony of the garden, the bitter Cross, and the grave—Christ bore them all for one great end: "that ye through his poverty might be rich." His great concern was to reach people of all classes, so he came among the poorest that he might be accessible to all. "Poor yet making many rich"—such was the life of Jesus on earth. When William Burns, a Scottish missionary, died in China, his converts round his bed looked for his property, that they might gather it together. They found an English and a Chinese Bible, a worn and much used writing case, a lantern, a single suit, and the blue flag of his Gospel boat. That was everything which the missionary owned. "He must have been very poor," a child whispered in the stillness of the room. He was very poor, but he made many rich. James Smetham, an artist in London and a Methodist class leader, tells in one of his letters of an old member of his class meeting. "He stumbled along on hot June days, with a tendency to hernia, selling a bit of tea, and with a pension, but when he came into his class meeting he prayed as if he had ten thousand a year." We are rich, not in what we have but in what we cannot lose.

The Incarnation was the temporary impoverishment of the Son of God for the everlasting enrichment of the sons of men. He came down to us that he might lift us up to himself. In this word "for your sake" is revealed the whole mystery of the passion of God for man. "Unto *us* a child is born, unto *us* a Son is given." "Unto *you* is born this day a Savior." He became poor for our sake. Dr. Inge used to say that the difference between a sermon and a lecture is that a sermon is addressed to individuals. It asks, How does this matter concern you? It has a searchingly personal quality. Has Christ enriched you that through his poverty you have become rich? How stands the case with you?

Unless we know the Lord Jesus as our Savior and Friend, unless we possess the unsearchable riches that he provides, we are poor indeed. The birth of Jesus is not only an event which happened in the past at a certain time and place. It is also an experience which is capable of unlimited repetition. If we want to carry the spirit of Christmas into the whole year, then Christ must be born anew in us, so that we may say with the apostle Paul, "Christ in me is the hope of glory."

EPIPHANY

III

Gifts from Heaven

Opening their treasures, they offered him gifts, gold and frankincense and myrrh.

Matthew 2:11 RSV

At Christmas, God sends us three gifts. They last forever, and they are sent to any who will receive them. Long before Jesus came, the Hebrews attached an almost sacramental significance to the giving of gifts. The dowry or "mohar", the love gift or "minha" implied the benevolent intent of the giver and the promised good faith of the receiver. To the infant Christ the wise men brought gold, the gift for a king; frankincense, the gift for a priest; and myrrh, the gift for one who was to die. So they foretold that the child in the manger was to be the true king, the perfect high priest, and in the end the supreme Savior of men.

When we accept God's Christmas gifts, our lives can be changed and our souls nurtured in their loving intent. The gift of God is eternal life—this is symbolized by the Christmas gifts he sends us from heaven. He sent the wise men a star, a new reason to look up. He sent the shepherds a song, a new reason to live. He sent all of us a Son, a new reason to love. Dr. P. T. Forsyth once said, "The gifts of God are not there to be looked at in the mouth, but to be lived in the heart."

1. God sent the wise men a star—a new reason to look up. For two hundred years before the Nativity there had been a widespread expectation of the coming of the Messiah. Men lived in a time of darkness, cruelty, oppression, and fear. No one knows exactly who the wise men were or from whence they came. The Armenian Gospel of the Infancy identifies them as Melchior (Light), king of Persia; Caspar (White), king of India; and Balthasar (Lord of the Treasury), king of Arabia. Whoever they were, they were tired of the superstition and ignorance and low moral standards of their time. They were clever, discerning men who were looking for a new revelation of wisdom.

By 500 B.C. Persians had the capacity to predict eclipses. Both Pliny and Suetonius, Roman historians, record that about fifty years before the birth of Christ a Persian astrologer named Tiridates came to Rome expressing Messianic expectations. In the early seventeenth century Kepler calculated that at about the time of our Lord's birth there was an astronomic conjunction of Mars, Saturn, and Jupiter. Alexander von Humboldt later confirmed this through careful evaluation of ancient Chinese celestial tables. For centuries the Star of Bethlehem has fascinated many of the world's keenest scientific minds. On behalf of New York's Planetarium, Catherine Barry has written an interesting pamphlet, "The Christmas Star." Whether the star was really a comet, a nova, an especially brilliant star, or a conjunction of the planets, we do not know. But we do know that the star was sufficiently unusual to capture the interest of the wise men and lead them eventually to Bethlehem. They were led out of the darkness of despair into the light of Christ's presence.

As they scanned the heavens they saw in the East the star. They read in the heavens the fulfillment of human hope.

They looked up and followed the gleam which broke in upon their studies, the light that never was on sea or land. They were students who were also seekers. They were on the alert, searching the skies and the records—the scientific men of their time, pondering the old and watching for the new. "When they saw the star they rejoiced with exceeding great joy." Of itself knowledge does not make men happy, but wisdom, applied knowledge of the principles of right living, does. As Paul says, "You are wise in Christ." When possessed of such wisdom, men can rejoice because they are assured of a destiny inside the purpose of God.

Marie Sklodowska sat one day in a classroom of the University of Warsaw and heard her professor say, "Some of you have stars at your fingertips." She was a girl with a good heart and a brilliant mind devoted to truth. As a scientific student at the Sorbonne in Paris she developed an uncanny skill in searching for truth. She fell in love with one of her teachers, Pierre Curie, whom she married, and together they searched for a new element. The way was long and rugged. They were laughed at and they almost starved. On the verge of admitting failure they walked into their laboratory one night to see their evaporation dishes aglow in the darkness. Their struggle and search were over. The stars at their fingertips, which had lured them on, they touched at last and found radium.

So the wise men had stars at their fingertips. They saw a star so remarkable in its brilliance and movement that they were willing to follow where it led. God was to them the mighty ruler of all things. They looked up to the night sky so that they might learn more of his purposes, believing that the very stars existed to be linked with the destinies of men.

When, with the wise men, we look up, we too see God's heavenly gift of a guiding star. In 1802 Nathaniel Bowditch published *The New American Practical Navigator*. In many ways this book remains unsurpassed as a guide to navigation. It stresses that stars travel in fixed and preditable patterns and that by following their fixed courses men can safely cross uncharted oceans. Today we are told that there are no absolute standards of right and wrong. We live in a permissive society. But the truth is that you will never get to Bethlehem unless you look up and, like the wise men, follow the star until you come to the Christ.

2. God sent the shepherds a song—a new reason to live. Until they heard the angels' song, the shepherds had little for which to live. The priests called them "dirt people" and classed them with thieves. The shepherds were despised by the orthodox good people of the day. They were unable, by reason of their work, to keep all the details of the ceremonial laws. They could not observe all the hand-washings and rules and regulations. Their flocks made far too constant demands on them, and so the orthodox looked down on them as very common people. The archaeologist Nelson Glueck says that on the average they lived about thirty to forty years. But the song the angels sang gave the shepherds a new and wonderful reason to live. "Glory to God in the highest, and on earth peace, good will toward men." The divine promise was distinctive. It recognized the Christ Child, and it was confirmative. It contained proof of the angels' statements.

According to the book of Job, when God laid the foundations of the earth, "The morning stars sang together, and all the sons of God shouted for joy" (Job 38:7). So now the same chorus gathers to celebrate the new creation, in which God's full glory will be displayed by the fulfillment of his eternal purpose and man's true peace will be realized by the establishment of God's kingdom.

A song can change your life and make it worth living. The angel's song can still overcome all the dull misery of a godless life. During the sixteenth century an incredibly brave people, the Huguenots, were sorely persecuted in France for their Protestant faith. Yet again and again, outnumbered and ill-equipped as they were, the Huguenots triumphed. Their secret weapon was a song. Their custom was to enter the field of battle singing the Psalms of David. The shepherds heard the angels' song, and all at once the apathy, the discouragement, and terror of life left them. They had a new reason to live.

3. God gave us all a Son—a new reason to love. In differing measure we can all share the sense of expectancy the wise men knew as they followed the star or the sense of exaltation the shepherds had when they heard the angels sing. But the truth of Christmas does not really become apparent to most of us until we accept God's Son, his unspeakable gift, and find in him a new reason to love. In Hebrew tradition the birth of a son was always an occasion of special rejoicing. The coming of a son gave hopes of stability, prosperity, and perpetuity to a tribe or a family. Jesus Christ was born in dire poverty, in an occupied country, to a peasant woman. But Mary and Joseph had a son to love, and they were ready to share him with the world. The Incarnation had taken place. The Word had become flesh and had begun to abide among men. In every generation men have found in Christ the continuity of God's saving grace. In Christ each one finds the type and example of the love that he most needs to have and to share.

In his account of his Asiatic travels Marco Polo tells of visiting a Persian village where he heard an unusual legend concerning the reactions of the wise men. The youngest saw in Christ the promise, beauty, and joy of youth; the middle-aged saw in him the enduring resilience of the good life; and the oldest saw in him the beginning of an eternity of which he would soon be a part. Each man finds in Christ the satisfaction of his deepest need. In him each one of us can see a special invitation and opportunity to love.

It is this coming of Jesus into life with all its joys and sorrows that brings him so near to us. He is Immanuel—God with us. He is with us all the days because he came to us on that first Christmas Day. "Surely he hath borne our griefs and carried our sorrows." (Isaiah 53:4) Jesus knew what it was to be weary and heavy laden and how to find rest in burdensome days, and so he can say, "Come to me, all ye that labor and are heavy laden and I will give you rest." He comes to children and bids them come to him; and they come, knowing that he is their friend. He comes to the publicans and sinners and bids them come to him; and they answer his call, for they know that he loves them.

He has come—God's greatest gift—and he says to us, "Come." He is the only one who invites us all, folk of all nations, for he is a light to lighten the Gentiles as well as the glory of his people Israel. We are all sinners, so he bids us all come to him. We surely will not repeat the great tragedy of his first coming, when "he came unto his own and they that were his own received him not." Rather will we say:

> I asked for Thee
> And Thou didst come
> To take me home
> Within Thy heart to be.

ASH WEDNESDAY

IV

Is Repentance Out of Date?

The time is fulfilled, and the kingdom of God is at hand; repent, and believe in the gospel.

Mark 1:15 RSV

"Repentance" is a word which rings through every part of the Bible from beginning to end. It was the burden of the preaching of the prophets, the apostles, and Christ himself. It sums up the gospel, for, after Christ had risen from the dead, he told his disciples to go forth and preach repentance and forgiveness of sins through his name. In our text are stated the two indispensable elements in all evangelism—repent and believe. Repent comes first, for you cannot believe unless you repent. The gospel cannot get into a man's mind and heart unless he first opens the door. But he never will open it unless we can make him see that in closing the door against the gospel he is shutting out his own highest life and at the same time defeating God's purpose for him.

"Repent" is the word that opens heaven, for only a forgiven sinner can enter heaven and only a sinner who repents can be forgiven. "Repent" is the word which brings a sinner back from the far country to his father's house. It is the word that brings joy to the angels. It is the word with which Jesus began to preach. It is the word with which Peter addressed the crowd on the day of Pentecost. It is the word which David spoke when the prophet Nathan rebuked him for his sin. It is the word which Peter uttered when he went out into the night and wept bitterly. It is the word that opened the gates of Paradise to the dying thief on the cross.

Repentance belongs to the very essence of the Christian faith. It is the first and last word of the soul's life—the last because our deepening knowledge of God will bring a deeper penitence to our latest hour, and the first because the first movement of the soul toward God is a sense of sin and a spirit of contrition. To repent means to change the direction we are going and to reorganize our lives. It means to find new values to live by and to confess that we have taken the wrong turn. It means to take a long look backward and find out where we went wrong. It humbles our pride and rebukes our complacency. It tells us that there is something radically wrong with our lives.

Repentance is not out of date. Jesus said "Unless you repent you will all . . . perish" (Luke 13:5 RSV). Repent is something everyone can do. We can will to be done with sin. We can will to turn to God. We can will to commit ourselves utterly to Christ. What we can do we must do. God will not do it for us. The risen Lord said to the church at Laodicea: "Those whom I love, I reprove and chasten; so be zealous and repent" (Revelation 3:19 RSV). When the crowd in Jerusalem at Pentecost heard Peter's sermon, they were cut to the heart and said to him, "What shall we do?" Peter replied, "Repent, and be baptized everyone of you in the name of Jesus Christ for the forgiveness of your sins" (Acts 2:37-38 RSV). Again after he had healed the lame man at the Beautiful gate of the Temple, Peter said, "Repent therefore, and turn again, that your sins may be blotted out" (Acts 3:19 RSV). Paul speaks of repentance and turning to God at Lystra to simple and superstitious people, at Athens to the intellectuals, and before King Agrippa.

Lent is a penitential season, a time for self-examination. So it is a fitting time for us to learn what true repentance means.

1. Repentance occurs in three stages. There is, to begin with, a burden on the back such as Bunyan's Pilgrim carried, a sense of guilt before God, a deep feeling of shame, regret and remorse for past wrongdoing. Everyone who looks into his own heart knows the accuracy of the words we often use when we repeat the General Confession. "We have left undone those things which we ought to have done, and we have done those things which we ought not to have done." Emerson once said, "We come to church properly for self-examination, to see how it stands with us." If I compare myself with those around me, I may have a fairly good opinion of myself but not when I reflect on the character of Jesus. In the light of that comparison I can only say with Peter, "Depart from me; for I am a sinful man, O Lord" (Luke 5:8). I can say of Jesus, even more truly than Shakespeare makes Iago say of Cassius, "He hath a daily beauty in his life that makes me ugly." When we measure ourselves, not by the easy standards of our fellows but by the law and thought of God, we see our need of repentance.

There is a very real sense in which the way to repentance is through self-loathing and self-disgust. To come to hate one's present way of life and one's present self is the path to a new way of life and a new self. O. Henry has a story of a young man who went from a little village to the great city. In the village he had been brought up in the innocence of a good home and a good school. In the city he took to petty crime and became a pickpocket and a confidence man. One day, just after he had picked someone's pocket, he saw a girl he had known and loved in the old village. She did not see him, but he saw her. She was just as fresh and sweet and innocent and pure as she had been. He looked at her in all her innocent purity. He looked at himself in all his cheap and tawdry crime. He leaned his head against a lamppost and said, "God, how I hate myself." That is the first step to repentance, the realization of what we are and the self-disgust which comes from that realization.

Remorse is not in itself repentance. People may deplore their shortcomings, be genuinely sorry for past sins, and be filled with remorse for the wrong they have done to themselves and to others. But if they stop there and take no further action, their sorrow is merely a sorrow unto death and not the godly sorrow that leads to repentance. The definition I learned as a boy from the Methodist Catechism is a sound one. "Repentance is true sorrow for sin *and* a sincere effort to forsake it."

2. This leads us to the second stage of repentance—a change of mind, which is the strict meaning of the original Greek word in the New Testament. The call to repentance is a call to change our outlook, to think differently about the way we are living, and to learn to see things through God's eyes and not our own. When Jesus preached in Galilee, his first word was "Repent, for the kingdom of God is at hand." In other words, Jesus is telling his hearers that a new age has dawned, a new order is coming to pass in which old things will pass away and all things will become new. T. H. Huxley defined life as "complete correspondence with our environment" and death as its opposite. If we are to live in this new world of values, then we must learn to adjust ourselves to the new order of things. To repent is to adopt God's viewpoint instead of our own. It means a complete

revaluation of all the things we are inclined to call good. To repent is to put on a new mind. It is not a mere feeling of sorrow or contrition for an act of wrongdoing. It is contrition not for what we do but for what we are in our nature. It is an activity of the whole personality. We are told of St. Jerome that one Christmas night he wished to offer his Lord his work on the Holy Scriptures, then his labor for the conversion of souls, then such virtues as he was able to offer. But this was not what the Lord wanted. "Jerome," he said; "It is thy sins I wished for: give them to me that I may pardon them." To hold the Christian faith you must repent of your sins. You can do no other if you have been captured by the love of Christ.

3. We not only need a new contrition and a new habit of thought; we also need a new direction. It is not enough to tell people to mourn over their sins, to alter their outlook, and set out on a new way; for in fact they lack the power to do so. Seneca, the Roman writer, says: "It is impossible for a man of himself to escape. It must be that someone shall stretch out a hand to help him up." So the gospel of repentance in the New Testament is never preached without that outstretched hand. Repentance unto life is always a repentance toward God. In the New Testament it is always linked with faith in God. All hope for the repentant sinner lies in his willingness to trust to that outstretched hand and trust it utterly. Even this willingness is itself the gift of grace. As Karl Barth has put it: "Repentance is not the best and finest and noblest achievement of the righteousness of man. It is the Word which God has written in man's heart and is from God, not man."

It is the consciousness of what our sin is to God, of the wrong it does to his holiness, of the wound which it inflicts on his love that leads to repentance. As David says,

IS REPENTANCE OUT OF DATE?

"Against thee, thee only, have I sinned and done this evil in thy sight." The prophet Hosea writes, "Come, let us return to the Lord; for he has torn, that he may heal us; he has stricken, and he will bind us up" (Hosea 6:1 RSV). Isaiah says, "Let the wicked forsake his way, and the unrighteous man his thoughts; let him return to the Lord, that he may have mercy on him, and to our God, for he will abundantly pardon" (Isaiah 55:7).

No road sign is more familiar on our highways than the sign "No U-turn," which means that turning completely around at this spot and going in the opposite direction is forbidden. But we find exactly the opposite in the Bible. "Make a U-turn." That is the meaning of the word "repent." In repentance we are turned right round away from sin and self and toward God. Saul of Tarsus made a U-turn when he ceased being Saul the persecutor and became Paul the apostle.

The only proof that repentance is real is the proof of an amended life. The consistent demand is for fruits which will match the repentance. So John the Baptizer said to the crowds who came into the desert to be baptized by him, "Bear fruit that befits repentance" (Matthew 3:8 RSV). So Paul said to King Agrippa, "I was not disobedient to the heavenly vision, but declared to [Jews] and also to the Gentiles, that they should repent and turn to God and perform deeds worthy of their repentance" (Acts 26:19-20 RSV). The repentance which is confined to words and to emotions is not real. The emotion of repentance has to be worked out in action. Words of repentance have to be guaranteed by amended deeds. Repentance is no easy, sentimental, emotional thing in which we say we are sorry and then go away and do the same thing over again. Repentance involves the humiliating experience of self-examination and the determination to be changed. Dean Inge tells of a Jew who said to him, "In our religion repentance means not 'grieve' but 'turn,' " and Inge comments, "I think when our Lord spoke of repentance he meant the same." Lady Julian of Norwich even says that for the saved soul his or her past faults are felt "no longer as wounds but as worships."

Lent ought to be a season of heart-searching and of true and entire repentance toward God. It is not necessary to put ashes on our heads in token of our penitence, as Gregory the Great made people do thirteen hundred years ago, from which custom Ash Wednesday gets its name. But it is necessary that we should "rend our hearts though not our garments." Penitence is the first condition on which men enter the kingdom of God and inherit life everlasting. Repentance needs to be renewed again and again, for the best of us are always slipping back and need a new contrition, a new habit of thought and a new direction. As Dr. Alexander Whyte used to say, "The perseverance of the saints consists in ever new beginnings."

> Come, let us to the Lord our God
> With contrite hearts return.
> Our God is gracious nor will leave
> The desolate to mourn.

FIRST SUNDAY IN LENT

V

The Snare of the Shortcut

When Pharaoh let the people go, God did not lead them by way of the land of the Philistines, although that was near; for God said, "Lest the people repent when they see war, and return to Egypt." But God led the people round by the way of the wilderness toward the Red Sea.

Exodus 13:17-18 RSV

There is a lure in the shortcut similar to that in the bargain. If we can cut a corner, if we can reach our destination a minute sooner or by a route a few yards shorter, we feel the same sort of pride in the achievement as when we have secured some article at a lower price than its market value. In many cases the shortcut is legitimate and useful. What sense is there in wasting time and effort? Every invention is a shortcut. The telephone, telegram, radio, automobile, airplane—all recommend themselves to us by the claim that they get us where we want to be more quickly.

But there are dangers in the shortcut. Sometimes it does not get us there at all. When Columbus discovered America it was by accident. He was seeking a new route, a shortcut to India. When he first sighted land, he thought it was India he had reached. His shortcut was a happy one for the world, but it was a failure from his point of view. That is often the fate of the man who tries the shortcut. He does not arrive. He aims for India and reaches America.

Even when the shortcut does take us to our destination it often proves to be a long way round. We waste time instead of saving it. Bunyan in the *Pilgrim's Progress* tells of Bypath Meadow, which seemed to Christian and Hopeful to be easier going than the narrow way; but they soon got lost and fell into the hands of Giant Despair. Many proverbs support this idea that the shortcut is a snare. "Haste makes waste." "More haste, less speed." "Look before you leap." "Think twice before you speak."

People take shortcuts to wealth—reckless speculation, gambling, dishonesty that keeps just within the law. In many cases the shortcut proves a deceitful snare. It does not lead to the golden gates. But even when it does, it is over broken hearts and ruined lives. There are shortcuts of this kind to pleasure. Indulgence has its joys, which may be quite innocent, but when the cost of them is another's pain or dishonor, the shortcut is the path of shame.

In education there are no shortcuts. Students sometimes cram for an examination. Cramming is a shortcut but it does not get there. It may succeed as far as the examination is concerned, but it does not lead to the culture which is the true end of study. Steady, persistent work, hard reading and thinking— that is the only way to culture. There is a great truth in Carlyle's definition of genius as "an infinite capacity for taking pains," though it is not a complete definition.

When we study God's methods as revealed in nature and history we notice how shy he is of shortcuts and how he prefers the long way round. How leisurely and patiently he seems to be working out his purposes. The earliest account of creation represents it as a shortcut. "And God said, Let there be—and there was." But we know now that creation was not the work of a moment but an age-long process.

THE SNARE OF THE SHORTCUT

Scientists look back millions of years and see the world slowly unfolding into new forms of beauty and life.

As in creation so it was in redemption. We often hear the question asked, "Why did not Jesus come earlier into the world?" What a long, weary wait humanity had for its Savior. The only satisfactory answer to that question is that given by Paul: "When the time had fully come, God sent forth his Son" (Galatians 4:4 RSV). The world had to be made ready for Jesus. The Jewish race had to be prepared by long discipline to produce the Messiah.

Our text tells us of one of the stages in the long road of discipline and preparation along which God led his chosen people. It is strange to think that by the straight road it was quite a brief journey from Egypt to Palestine. Four or five days of marching would have brought the children of Israel to the Promised Land. Yet they took forty years to do it. We know the hardships and the sorrows and the struggle that filled with bitterness those forty years. Yet, for all that, the leadership was God's. The longest way round proved the shortest way home.

It is not difficult for us to see God's reasons for this roundabout way, as George H. Morrison has pointed out in one of his sermons. The Bible lifts the veil for us a little, and we find, first, that there was compassion in it. That near way was through the land of the Philistines, who were skilled in the arts of war. They were the strongest enemies whom the children of Israel had to meet. It was surely according to the highest wisdom, therefore, that they should meet the Philistines last. For, remember, the children of Israel had been in slavery for two hundred years. A slave cannot be made a free man in a day. He has the mind of a slave long after his chains have been unloosed. He needs to learn that he is free, that he is able to act for himself. And he can learn this only slowly. Such were the Israelites when they broke from Egypt. We can hear the voices of men who were still slaves in spirit in such a cry as "Would it not be better for us to return to Egypt?" To have brought this rabble of undisciplined slaves face to face with the Philistines might have ended in disaster and sent them headlong back to Egypt. The time was coming when the armies of Israel would be more than a match for the hosts of the Philistines, but that time was not yet. So God led them by another way—by a way on which they would meet no enemies for a time. It was surely an act of compassion so to lead the people that they should not be discouraged at the beginning of their new life. It took forty years to change the rabble into a disciplined army. It was a roundabout road, but it was the right road for all that.

But there was more than compassion in it: there was education. Can you realize what the world would have lost if Israel had been allowed to take the shortcut? Five days might have brought them to Canaan but still with Egypt and bondage in their blood. It took one night to take Israel out of Egypt, someone has said, but it took forty years to take Egypt out of Israel. When I think of all that Israel learned in that devious journey, when I remember how it enriched and deepened their knowledge of themselves and of their God, I feel that the purpose of God was in it.

Only by such a long way of discipline could they hope to become equal to the tasks and responsibilities that were to be theirs. Even promised lands have to be won, and undisciplined slaves win no conquests. The first task was to change slaves into men. Laws had to be framed and obedience slowly taught. Shortcuts are no good for such a great task as that. The roundabout way was the only possible way of achieving God's great plan. "God led them

THE SNARE OF THE SHORTCUT 43

not through the way of the Philistines, though that was near." They were disappointed, as men often have been who expected God to take the swift and direct way.

In the first century, Christians expected the speedy return of our Lord. They were a bitterly persecuted people. The Roman Empire did its best to stamp them out. There was a cry from the depths of their hearts, "O Lord, how long?" It was a prayer for the swift overthrow of the forces of evil. But their hope was disappointed then, and it has been for nearly two thousand years since. The history of Christianity, all the wonder and romance of it, has come out of the disappointment of that hope. The reading of history shows that so far the Divine way has been the roundabout way.

Slowly but surely God's purposes of grace are maturing, and he is guiding all things to their goal. But he is not straining or forcing events. He has long patience. At the opening of his ministry our Lord was assailed by the temptation to take a shortcut. It was a real temptation, a temptation natural to one who had just seen a vision of his future mission. It was just after the baptism in Jordan that Jesus was tempted. Evil often catches us after some exalted moment. "The devil took him to a very high mountain, and showed him all the kingdoms of the world and the glory of them; and he said to him, 'All these I will give you, if you will fall down and worship me'" (Matthew 4:8-9 RSV).

Jesus recognized at once that this was a suggestion from the devil and he rejected it. "No shortcuts for me," he said. "I will take the long road that God points out for me. I will win the world by love and love alone." This temptation kept on coming to Jesus in the days that followed. Both friends and foes urged him to take the shortcut. His followers would more than once have made him a king. If he had been willing to exploit the enthusiasm of the people and accommodate himself to their ideas, he might easily have had a kingdom of sorts, but it would have passed away as speedily as it had come. But Jesus refused. He took the roundabout way, which led to a place called Calvary. By that route he came to the Name that is above every name.

All good men are eager for the coming of God's kingdom. But we want it to come too easily. We want God to take a shortcut to win the world to himself. "Thy Kingdom come," we pray.

> O, what long, sad years have gone
> Since thy church was taught this prayer,
> O, what eyes have watched and wept
> For its dawning everywhere.
>
> —John Page Hopps

Yes, it is a long road and we need patience to keep trudging along the way with a heart that never tires because we see with the eyes of God. In Richard Coupland's life of William Wilberforce there are some very suggestive chapter headings: "The Call," "Novitiate," "Crusade," "Check," "Interruption," "Persistence," "Victory." Like all great reforms, the abolition of the slave trade took longer than the reformers had thought, and the end is not yet. "We began to perceive," said Wilberforce, "more difficulties in the way than we had hoped there would be." Year after year he brought in his resolutions, and they were defeated. Yet something was happening in that roundabout way. Public opinion was coming to see that slavery itself was only less abominable than the slave trade. So the roundabout road prepared the way for a greater moral triumph than the shortcut.

There is no greater test of our faith and endurance than these roundabout ways. But let us remember the promise of

THE SNARE OF THE SHORTCUT

our Lord: "In your patience you shall win your soul." God's thoughts are long, long thoughts. He cares as much for the going as for the goal. As Dr. John Oman has pointed out, "Man makes the straight canal: God makes the winding rivers," and we must learn of the patience of God. "Rest in the Lord, and wait patiently for him. . . . He shall give thee the desires of thine heart" (Psalm 37:7,4), all that we deeply wish, all that God has wished for us from the foundation of the world.

God's main purpose with us is not to get us somewhere but to make something of us on the way. The Israelites learned more on their way to the Promised Land than they ever learned anywhere else. It is the struggle and the character developed in that struggle that matters. There is no shortcut to goodness. Conversion may be sudden; but conversion is not the end, it is only the beginning. The new life thus begun has to grow into maturity. Even of our Lord it is recorded that he was made perfect through suffering. There is no shortcut to any of the graces that make up Christian character. If you want to reach that Canaan, you must go round by way of the wilderness. When your way is rough and lonely, when you are beaten by failure and chilled with disappointment, remember that God is seeking to develop your soul by those experiences. The big thing in life is the growth of the soul. It is not getting somewhere or finding something on which we have set our hearts that matters. It is what we become on the way that counts. Though your way be roundabout, full of mistakes and struggle, hold to it even in the dark and go ahead, for God will be with you all the way, and at last you will emerge, in his good time, into the land flowing with milk and honey.

PASSION SUNDAY

VI

Why Is God Silent?

My God, my God, why hast thou forsaken me? Why art thou so far from helping me, and from the words of my roaring?

Psalm 22:1

It is never an easy task to justify the ways of God to men. When Paul declares that they are past tracing out, he speaks for us all. One thing which is hard for us to understand is the apparent silence of God in the face of the evil of the world. There is a time to keep silence and a time to speak. But surely it is the time to speak when evil is openly done among men. Yet how often in such circumstances God seems dumb. The wicked pursue their course unchecked: wrongdoing flaunts itself without restraint. Man's inhumanity to man calls out for redress, and yet God does nothing. "My God, my God, why hast thou forsaken me?" None can plumb the depths of that cry of dereliction from the Cross. But it suggests that the silence of God in such an hour lay heavily on the spirit of Jesus.

The writers of the Psalms continually express their bewilderment before the silences of God. Many of these songs came out of troubled times, when the nation and its leaders were beset with difficulties. "Why does God stand afar off?" they asked; "Why does he keep silent?" "How

WHY IS GOD SILENT?

long wilt thou forget me, O Lord? For ever? How long wilt thou hide thy face from me?" (Psalm 13:1). "O God, do not keep silence; do not hold thy peace or be still, O God!" (Psalm 83:1 RSV). When nothing happened and the heavens were as brass above them, they cried out, "Verily thou art a God that hidest thyself" (Isaiah 45:15).

This is true in our own experience. We sometimes seem to cry to a vacant heaven. Our need is urgent, but there is no message from God. The experience of God's silence is so common that it accounts more than anything else for the disappointment so many people feel in regard to religion. We can understand the meaning of that verse in one of F. W. Faber's hymns, which says of God:

> He hides himself so wondrously
> As though there were no God.
> He seems to leave us to ourselves
> Just when we need him most.

What are we to make of it? Why does God not answer? Does he really care? Does he even hear? "Thou didst hide thy face," says a psalmist; "I was troubled." Does God hide his face? Does he withdraw his comforts? Yes, he does. Though we call God "Father" we need not shrink from such a conclusion. He may have a purpose concerning us that can be fulfilled in no other way. God has his silences as well as his speech, times when he withdraws himself as well as times when he gives himself without stint to the soul.

But when we say that God hides his face and is silent, that does not mean that he abandons us. He is there all the time, though we may not see him. God's silence may draw us closer to him, deepening our sense of dependence, making us realize that without him we can do nothing. There are three different explanations men have offered to account for the silence of God—it is the silence of absence, of impotence, and of indifference.

1. *The silence of absence.* Men think of God as an absentee God, one who has wound up the universe as a clockmaker might wind up a clock and has left it to go on its own or to run down. His silence is the silence of detachment from the human scene. The story of Elijah confronting the prophets of Baal on Mount Carmel is rich in meaning here. The test—"The God who answers by fire, he is God"—had failed. "But there was no voice, and no one answered." Elijah's mocking comment was inevitable. "Cry aloud, for he is a god; either he is musing, or he has gone aside, or he is on a journey, or perhaps he is asleep and must be awakened" (I Kings 18:27 RSV). The soul can put no trust in an absentee God.

You remember the reproach that Martha addressed to Jesus after the death of Lazarus. "Lord, if you had been here, my brother would not have died" (John 11:21 RSV). "If you had been here—but you were not here." All down the ages during dark days people have wondered whether the Lord had forgotten to be gracious. One psalmist, speaking of the tyranny of his enemies, cried with impatience, "Lord, how long wilt thou look on?" (Psalm 35:17). Another says: "[Men] continually say unto me, Where is thy God?" (Psalm 42:3). Dr. Fosdick tells us that in a Danish Protestant church well on into the last century, worshipers maintained the custom of bowing when they passed a certain spot on the wall. The reason, which no one knew, was discovered when removal of the whitewash revealed a Roman Catholic Madonna. The worshipers in that church had been bowing for three centuries before the place where the Madonna used to be. So today many people worship God not as a present reality but as a tradition. Their faith is directed not toward the living God but toward what someone else has written about a God who used to be alive.

They feel that God is silent now because he is absent. They are like Gideon, who, when the divine messenger came and said, "The Lord is with you, you mighty man of valor," replied, "If the Lord is with us, why then has all this befallen us? And where are all his wonderful deeds which our fathers recounted to us?" (Judges 6:12-13 RSV).

Evelyn Underhill in one of her letters says: "As to God's absence it is of course illusion: it is he who casts the shadow that distresses you so." God is on the field when he is most invisible. We cannot think that God belongs only to the past. The present and the future also belong to him, who is the same yesterday, today, and forever.

2. *The silence of impotence.* This is the second explanation that has been offered to account for the silence of God. God is in the world, present but powerless. He either will not or cannot do anything. People ask, Why doesn't God do something? Why does he not intervene to bring the wicked to nought? Why does he permit iniquity to waste the world? Is he powerless to help? Not long before Thomas Carlyle's death, his friend James Anthony Froude said to him that he could only believe in a God who did something. "With a cry of pain that I shall never forget he replied, 'God just sits there and does nothing.' " Many people feel exactly as Carlyle felt. They have no doubt that if God could arrest evil and stem the tide of iniquity, he would do so. His love, they argue, would insist upon it, but he lacks the power. The might of evil is greater than the power of God. The world has got out of hand and beyond God's power to control it.

Think of the arrogance which is displayed in this attitude to God. We take it for granted that we are capable of understanding everything that God does. We question God's actions in precisely the same way as we question the actions of our fellows. God is to conform to *our* ideas and do what *we* believe he ought to do. But our arrogance does not stop there. It does not hesitate to condemn God's actions and to say that they are quite wrong, as though we were the final court of appeal. But his thoughts are not ours, neither his ways. As Paul says: "Who are you, a man, to answer back to God? Will what is molded say to its molder, 'Why have you made me thus?'" (Romans 9:20 RSV).

God has given us freedom because he wants us to be not slaves but sons, not machines but men. It is a great risk that he has taken. The whole creation has been groaning in travail together until now, says Paul, in order that God may bring many sons to glory. But God did not create us as free agents and leave us to make our own choice, while he looked on as a mere spectator. He is not outside the world but in it. In ways that are hidden from us he is working with those who do battle for righteousness. "His love is as great as his power and neither knows measure nor end."

3. *The silence of indifference.* This is the third explanation that people have offered to account for the silence of God. Tennyson's phrase, "on the hills like gods together, careless of mankind," exactly represents many people's idea of God. They think of him as a vague figure who gave this toboggan of a universe its first push and has not thought seriously about it since. A wanderer down the street might put a child on his sled and start him going down hill and then go on his way. The child might fall off, but the wanderer will not care: there may be a tragic accident but that will not be his concern; he has gone away down the street. Many nominal believers have a God like that, who is uninterested in the welfare of his people and unmoved by their sorrows and

suffering. A God who does not care does nor count. But we know that God does care. Even in the Old Testament we can learn that, for does not the prophet Hosea represent God as saying: "How can I give you up, O Ephraim! How can I hand you over, O Israel!" (Hosea 11:8 RSV). "In all their afflictions he was afflicted," and to make us quite sure that he does care, God sent his only Son to die upon the Cross. Is any suffering like his suffering; is any sorrow to be compared to his?

None of these explanations that we have considered really explains the silence of God. His is not the silence of absence, of impotence, or of indifference, but in Whittier's phrase "the silence of eternity interpreted by love." There is a beautiful word in the prophecy of Zephaniah which, translated literally from the Hebrew, reads: "He will be silent in his love" (Zephaniah 3:17). There are silences of love as well as speech. There are times when love must say nothing and do nothing. Our opportunities lie sometimes in the silences of God. As we look back over the years we see that it was well that God did not heed our eager cries for interference.

The silence of God is part of his gracious discipline that seeks our spiritual maturity. It springs out of his patience with our waywardness and folly. Our Lord had to keep many things from his disciples. He had to be silent in his love for them. "I have many things to say unto you but you cannot bear them now." But he also said, "If it were not so, I would have told you." The silence of love, the fact that God does not as a rule interfere in any outward way, has developed our characters. He gives us enough light to carry us through. He gives us a lamp, though it be only to our feet: the darkness remains round about.

How eloquent is the silence of God! His silence in the face

of wrong is the silence of one who has spoken, who has finally declared himself and has no further need of words. He has spoken to us in his Son. Christ is the word of God, especially Christ crucified. The Cross of Christ was God's last word in the face of human wrong, and the silence that followed is full of expression.

In the garden of Gethsemane Jesus prayed that the cup might pass from him, but it did not. When he hung upon the Cross men mocked saying, "Let God deliver him now, if he delight in him," and nothing happened. From the Cross rings out an awful cry, "My God, my God, why hast thou forsaken me?" and only silence brooded over Calvary. God spoke no word, and yet he was there, and his was the silence of love. Love was silent there because love was suffering for the redemption of the world. God was silent because he was on the Cross making peace. The Cross speaks of God's love for the sinner and his repudiation of his sin. That is what the Cross says, and the silence that has followed confirms it. It is a speaking silence: let us hear it and obey. It is a waiting silence: let us arise and go to the Father. But it is not an endless silence. "God is not dumb that he should speak no more." Our God shall come and shall not keep silence. And when he speaks, he shall be justified. He will be clear when he judges. It is the sinner who will be silent in that day, without one plea, self-condemned for the silence of God which he would not hear, no less than for the word of God which he would not obey. As Ignatius finely says: "He who has the word of Jesus for a true possession can also hear his silence." And hearing Jesus we also hear the Father, and are assured that the silence of heaven is not the silence of absence, of impotence, or of indifference but the silence of eternity interpreted by love.

PALM SUNDAY

VII

The Colt That Carried a King

Tell the daughter of Zion, Behold your king is coming to you, humble, and mounted on an ass, and on a colt, the foal of an ass.

Matthew 21:5 RSV

If it were not for its sacred associations the picture of the King of kings entering his capital city on a donkey would be grotesque to modern minds. But we must remember that in the East the donkey was and is a real friend of the poor. He often proves more useful than the horse. He is sure-footed and can pick his way easily over narrow rocky paths and plod patiently up and downhill carrying quite heavy burdens. Men would ride to work on a donkey and use it in plowing the fields, threshing the corn, and carrying home the harvest.

There is a story in the Old Testament about a donkey that was wiser than its master, Balaam, though he was a prophet. He set out on its back to travel a long way to do something which was foolish and wrong. Several times the donkey stopped and did its best to end the expedition. Once it turned into a field. Then it went sideways into a wall and crushed the rider's foot. The third time it deliberately fell down with its master still on its back. The angry prophet whipped the ass, and it opened its mouth and protested. In short, when Balaam turned ass, the ass turned prophet, and it was only then that Balaam awoke to the presence of the angel of God standing in the way, blocking the road, so that Balaam should refrain from his wrongdoing. This was not the first time in history that a man has proved less intelligent and less sensitive to spiritual influences than an ass. Travelers in the East say that an ass is never taken in by a desert mirage.

At the beginning of our Lord's life it was an ass that carried him from Bethlehem into safety in Egypt when Herod ordered the slaughter of the innocents. So at the end of his life that humble animal emerges again, and Jesus deliberately chooses to ride on a colt, the foal of an ass, into Jerusalem. What was the significance of his choice and use of this animal on his triumphal entry into the Holy City?

1. In the first place, he meant it to be an assertion of his kingliness. There was a tradition among the Jews that when their Messiah came he would do so riding upon an ass. You find Zechariah saying: "Rejoice greatly, O daughter of Zion! Shout aloud, O daughter of Jerusalem! Lo, your king comes to you; triumphant and victorious is he, humble, and riding on an ass, on a colt the foal of an ass" (9:9 RSV). Such was the popular expectation in the time of Jesus. Our Lord, knowing this, makes use of it. Thus quietly does he claim to be the promised one, the King of the Jews. He is so sure of his triumph that he celebrates it before achieving it. He has such faith in the ultimate vindication of his cause that when the shadow of the Cross is upon him he sees the crown. The chief priests are planning to kill him; yet he rides into the city as a king. It is as though he were saying to the world,

THE COLT THAT CARRIED A KING

"Do your very worst: try me, condemn me, scourge me, crucify me: I will come out of it triumphant." Here was a faith daring enough to celebrate victory before the battle had been fought. Jesus showed by that inner certainty he possessed that his kingdom cannot fail.

In our text Jesus is described as sitting upon an ass and a colt, the foal of an ass. Now, of course, that was impossible. Our Lord was no circus rider. He must have chosen one of those beasts to ride upon, not both. The other Gospels clearly indicate that it was the colt he chose. He elected to sit upon an animal whereon never before man had sat, not upon one that had long been used in burden-bearing and that had often carried its master to the marketplace. In other words, Jesus here makes claim not only to belong to a race of kings, but to be a special king, unique and apart. He lifts himself into a solitary supremacy by choosing a beast that had never been ridden before. Later on, the dead body of the Master was given a unique tomb, we are told, wherein before no man was laid. But here Jesus chooses a unique throne. What is good enough for other men is not good enough for him. He demands a new place never occupied by any forerunner.

Are you willing to give that foremost place to Jesus in your life? In his letter to the Colossians, Paul uses this phrase, "that in everything he might be pre-eminent" (1:18 RSV). Are you willing to subscribe to that and to say, "There is no other interest in my life that I will place on an equal footing with my one Lord and master?" He demands that we should crown him as our rightful, lawful King. An Oxford lady of the intellectual type once said to Dr. Benjamin Jowett, the Master of Balliol College, Oxford, at a dinner party, "What do you think of Jesus Christ?" Dr. Jowett replied, "Madam, that is not the question. The question is, what does Jesus Christ think of me?" Jesus says to us now, "Will you accept me as your King? Will you give me the triumph I deserve and the hosannas that are my due?"

Someday, if not today, you will awake to the fact that Christ is unique, that he cannot be confined to the category of genius or of hero. If sin comes into your life or if sorrow visits your home, then you will discover that there is no other name given under heaven by which you can be saved. But why wait for that dark hour to come upon you? Why not take Christ at his own valuation now and give him the royal place that he desires?

2. In the second place, by his choice of the colt, Jesus intended to indicate not only the fact but the nature of his kingliness. "Your king is coming to you, humble, and mounted on a colt." Jesus chose the colt to emphasize his lowliness. Nothing declares more convincingly the claim of Jesus to be meek and lowly of heart than his entrance into Jerusalem on a colt. A military monarch entering the city would have ridden on a war horse. A merchant magnate would have had as his steed some noble Arabian horse, but Jesus rode in on a shaggy colt. At best it was a borrowed steed, obtained only on condition of its immediate return, and its trappings were the torn and weather-stained garments of peasants and fishermen.

It seems to me that if the crowds that day hailed Jesus as Messiah it cannot have been on account of any pomp or ceremonial connected with the occasion but because of some shining quality inherent in Jesus himself, a kingliness of bearing and character, which for all his humility could not be hid. Blaise Pascal, in a brilliant passage, compares emperors and conquerors of his day with Archimedes, who fought no battles but made certain discoveries that have contributed much to the world. He says of him, "though he did not catch the eye, how he blazed before the mind." Those words are still truer of Jesus. His kingliness is that of a quiet and meek and forgiving spirit, the kingliness of the Prince of Peace. His weapons are humility and gentleness and love.

Religions have been spread by force of arms before now. Military conquest accounts in large measure for the way in which Islam has covered a large part of the world. But this King will have nothing of that. His followers must be able to say with the Psalmist: "Some trust in chariots, and some in horses: but we will remember the name of the Lord our God" (Psalm 20:7). Only the Jews, of all the peoples of the ancient world, conceived their early heroes as men of peace. Other nations cherished stories of their famous men, and always they were men of war. Among the Norsemen we have the mighty Vikings. In England we find the stories of King Arthur and the Knights of the Round Table. The Romans, Indians, and Japanese all tell the story of their early warlike heroes. But among the Jews, Abraham, Isaac, and Jacob were friends of God and lovers of peace. Isaac and Jacob never went to war at all. Abraham fought only once, and he was forced into it; and though he conquered he took none of the spoil. It was this which affected the Hebrew hope of the Messiah. The ideal man of the Jews was a man of peace, and when the Messiah came he could come in the accouterments of peace, not on a prancing war horse but meekly riding upon a colt.

3. Finally, I would ask you to notice that Jesus chose a colt, not only to indicate the fact of his kingliness and its nature but also to show its method and its measure. Just think of what that colt was like—shaggy and untrained, very different from its amiable mother that ambled so easily by its side. Yet that was the means Jesus chose to demonstrate his

kingliness and his humility. The most foolish nature, the most coltish and undisciplined temperament, may be so used and transformed by Christ as to lose its lightness and frivolity and to become of signal service to him. Dr. W. E. Sangster sees a parable in that: "Whatever Christ touched he dignified, and no matter how despised a person or creature may be, Christ has a use for him."

Christ can use the ill-educated. John Bunyan the tinker, William Carey the shoemaker, William Booth the pawnbroker's assistant, were all intelligent men but lacked a formal education. They were scorned because of that, but what an influence they exerted. Christ can use the disfigured, like Henry Martyn with his wart-covered face and his stammer and George Whitefield with his squint. They were the subjects of cheap jokes, but Christ used them mightily for the extension of his kingdom.

Look back on history and note the hours when Christ has come in triumph, and you will see that in countless instances he has ridden in on a shaggy colt. For his disciples he did not go to the Pharisees, who were eminently respectable and safe, but to men like Simon Peter, men who were rough and ready and impulsive; not men who were broken in, but men who were ready to break out on a world which must be won from sin. Think of the Reformation when Christ came back in triumph to his own. Erasmus for all his cleverness and scholarship would never have brought about the Reformation unaided. It needed the son of a miner, "grand, rough old Martin Luther," as Robert Browning called him, to rend the petrified dignity of medieval Christendom. So in the eighteenth century in England, Christ took George Whitefield from behind the bar of the Bell Inn in Gloucester to be his evangelist. Let us take this for our comfort that Christ wants and can make use

THE COLT THAT CARRIED A KING

of the humblest, the most obscure and quaint among us.

There was once a road-sweeper in India, one of the outcastes, an untouchable, as they were called, but Christ found him and touched him and made use of him. He became a street preacher of great power. People would stand and listen to him and say, "There is something in him that we have not got." At last one day someone from the crowd said. "Why do they listen so respectfully to you who are only a sweeper?" This was his reply: "When my Savior was going to Jerusalem riding upon an ass, the people brought clothes and palm-branches and spread them under his feet. They did not spread them under the feet of Christ but under the feet of an ass. Why do that for an ass? Because the King of kings was riding upon that ass. When the Christ got down from it nobody cared about it. That ass was honored so long as the King of kings was riding upon it."

Will you allow Christ to take control of your life today? Will you set him in the saddle? If you will, there will come into your life an interest, a beauty, a fragrance, and a fruitfulness which you have never known before; and Jesus will enable you to do great things for him, whereof you will be glad. So say to him this day in the words of Philip Doddridge:

> My gracious Lord, I own thy right
> To every service I can pay
> And call it my supreme delight
> To hear thy dictates and obey.

MAUNDY THURSDAY

VIII

The Upper Room

He will show you a large upper room furnished and ready; there prepare for us.

Mark 14:15 RSV

The Gospels do not contain a more winsome story than that of the Upper Room. Jesus came up to Jerusalem with the multitude to keep the feast, knowing that he himself was to be the Passover Lamb. He was suspected, slandered, and harassed all the Holy Week. While the poorest of the people had a room of some kind in which to celebrate the great deliverance, he, of whom it all spoke, had no roof over his head. But he gave orders to his disciples as though every house in Jerusalem were open to him. He spoke as if there was an understanding between him and some secret acquaintance they did not know.

He tells two of his disciples to go into the city, where they will meet a man bearing a pitcher of water. This would be an unusual sight, for this was a woman's task. They are to follow him, and he will lead them to one described as the goodman of the house, probably the father of John Mark. We may imagine the two disciples passing through the city gate. A man lifts a jar on to his shoulders, looks at the two men and they at him, and a gleam of understanding passes between them. He turns his back on them and climbs up the steep way into the heart of the city. Soon he turns down a narrow lane, looks around to see if they are following, then passes across the courtyard of a house to where the goodman is waiting. The disciples give the password: "The Teacher says, Where is my guest room, where I am to eat the Passover with my disciples?" He shows them a large upper room, furnished and ready, and the disciples enter and begin to prepare the meal.

We must try to picture this room, for it was the first Christian church. It is the room where the Holy Communion was instituted and the room to which the disciples returned after the horror of the Crucifixion. It is the room whose doors were shut for fear of the Jews and in which Jesus appeared after his resurrection. It is the room which was swept, as with a mighty rushing wind, at Pentecost. It is the room to which Peter fled after his deliverance from prison. A church soon grew up on the site of this house and became known as the Coenaculum, a word that suggests *coena*, the Latin word for the dining hall: it survived the destruction of Jerusalem in A.D. 70.

The most impressive feature of the Coenaculum is its simplicity. One reaches it by mounting an outer stone stairway, walking along a balcony, and stooping through a narrow door. It is a large, empty, plain room, the ceiling arched and supported by pillars and with a simple bronze tablet on the wall. To stand in this room as I did some years ago and read from the New Testament and lead a party of pilgrims in prayer is a profound religious experience. In the cool hushed atmosphere one felt the unmistakable presence of Christ.

There would be no chairs in the room, only soft divans or cushions placed on three sides. The guests keep their hats on but take off their shoes and comfortably recline on the divans. On the low table before them there are no forks, knives, or spoons. At the first celebration, the Passover was eaten in haste, with loins girded, with shoes on, and staffs in hand; but at the time we are describing, they had discarded the travelers' garments for festive robes and they had adopted the reclining posture at table, to show they were free men.

So we read that, at the Last Supper, the disciple whom Jesus loved was reclining on Jesus' lap. In the center of the couch at the top—the place of the head of the family—Jesus would be sitting, with John on his right hand and Judas on his left. Luke reports Jesus as saying a significant thing: "I have earnestly desired to eat this passover with you before I suffer" (Luke 22:15). He wanted to preserve this last evening with them, to make one last effort to bare his mind and purpose to them, to have their presence and company, but above all to give them those symbols of his body and blood which, ever since, more than any other spiritual means, have brought life to the souls of men.

The fourth Evangelist records at this point the washing of the disciples' feet, which Dr. James Hope Moulton called "the neglected sacrament." Can we imagine that feet-washing, in which majesty and humility meet? Jesus does the work of a slave. His hands touch the feet of the traitor and Judas knows that the Master knows what he intends to do. There was the baring of the heart of love and the answering glint of cold steel in the eyes of Judas. It was Christ's last effort to win Judas. To this end he tells his secret that he knows one of them will betray him. So incredible is this that each one can only think of himself—"Lord, is it I?" they ask, which is evidence of a fine loyalty within that group. Jesus lifts his eyes to look at Judas and knows that he

THE UPPER ROOM

has failed. To understand what follows we must bear in mind that there were two swords in the room, which Jesus afterward bade them take when they went to Gethsemane and also that what Jesus said to John—"It is he to whom I shall give this morsel when I have dipped it" (John 13:26 RSV)—was unheard by anyone else. Jesus had only to say to the disciples, "That is the man," and Peter's sword would not have tarried. Judas would never have left the room alive. Twelve men would have left the room to bury a comrade in the dark. Jesus would have kept his life and lost it. We might never have heard of him.

Jesus got Judas out of the room at the cost of his own life. He said to him, "What you are going to do, do quickly, ... He immediately went out; and it was night" (John 13:29, 30 RSV). What a world of horror is summed up in those simple words, "it was night." After supper Jesus took a loaf, blessed it and broke it and gave it to his disciples and said, "Take, eat, this is my body." Then he took a cup and when he had given thanks he gave it to them and they drank of it and he said, "This is my blood of the new covenant which is shed for many." Luke and Paul add that Jesus said, "This do in remembrance of me." It was probably after this that Jesus spoke to them along the lines of the teaching given in the fourteenth and fifteenth chapters of John's Gospel. Then they sang a hymn and went out into the garden.

The persistence of this Feast of Remembrance is one of the miracles of religious history. It has taken many forms and has been overlaid with varying degrees of ceremonial splendor, but it has survived. The Upper Room has enlarged itself, and multitudes of people in this as in every age can testify that when this feast is spread they find themselves nearer to their Lord than at any other time. Christ is known in the breaking of the bread.

It is amazing how much of himself our Lord puts into these simple symbols. Symbols are a very important part of our lives. We respect and revere our symbols—the flag, a coat of arms, a fraternity pin, a wedding ring. By themselves these symbols mean very little, but we cherish them for the associations and the love that they represent. It is not the symbols themselves but the reality behind them that counts. As Dr. John Oman puts it: "A symbol is an interpretation of the heart."

The bread is broken, the wine is poured out. Christ comes on the scene, and how much he brings with him. He brings his holy Incarnation, for he says, "This is my body: this is my blood." Body and blood—that is Incarnation. With these symbols in our hands we cannot forget that the Word was made flesh. We see before us real substances which represent real manhood. Christ brings with him his Cross and Passion, for the bread is broken and the wine poured out. Unless we are blind we can see through these things the thorns, the nails, the spear, the self-surrender, the darkness of the desolation, the completeness of the sacrifice. Christ brings with him his covenant. "This cup is the new covenant in my blood." A covenant is an agreement. It is something that brings people together. This sacrament is a bond of friendship between heaven and our own souls.

The broken bread, the poured out wine—these things are as simple and familiar as can be, but in them the temporal unveils the eternal. We look through them, and we see the Christ coming to meet us. The Incarnate Christ with his body and blood, the Atoning Christ with his body broken and his blood shed, the Christ of the ages, bearing in his hands the covenant which makes all things new.

We believe in the real presence of Christ at the table, for we describe the service as Holy Communion. We do not commune with a symbol or with a memorial: we commune with a Presence. We believe in a real Presence because we believe in a living Christ who has risen from the dead and who, though we cannot see him, encounters us spiritually as we use this means of grace which he has provided. Wonderful sacrament to be the drama and vehicle of so much, and yet more wonderful Savior to whom in this act of worshipful remembrance goes forth all our love and praise, as it was in the beginning, is now and ever shall be until the table is spread for the marriage supper of the Lamb. We may sum it up in the words of a great Scottish churchman, Dr. Robert Rainy: "What Christ will be to you in time is set forth in the bread and wine. What Christ will be to you in eternity earth has no symbols to declare."

The Upper Room has been called the dynamo-house of the New Testament, the great generating station whence come our supplies of light and power. The ancients believed that when the winds blew it was because the gods loosed them from caves where they were kept. It is true to say that God sends forth the winds of his Spirit from the Upper Room. For where else, except at the foot of the Cross, do we learn so much or find the weight and weariness of the world so lightened? Yet so many people seem to lose the Upper Room out of their lives. They never climb the stair and so they know neither its fellowship nor its wisdom. If we have not an upper room in our lives, shall we not set about making one? For if we furnish a guestchamber for Jesus, he will become our Host and we his guests.

> He now stands knocking at the door
> Of every sinner's heart.
> The worst need keep him out no more
> Or force him to depart.

Come quickly in, Thou Heavenly Guest,
Nor ever hence remove,
But sup with us and let the feast
Be everlasting Love.

—Charles Wesley

GOOD FRIDAY

IX

The Cross and the Garden

Now in the place where he was crucified there was a garden.

John 19:41 RSV

To the writers of the first three Gospels the Cross was a thing of unrelieved horror, but the writer of the Fourth Gospel saw deeper. He shows the glory shining through the gloom and is the only one to tell us of the garden near the Cross. We read in the Scriptures of many gardens. It was in a garden that the Bible placed man first, thereby signifying his innocence. "And the Lord God planted a garden in Eden, in the east; and there he put the man whom he had formed" (Genesis 2:8 RSV). The beauty of the surroundings was meant to be appropriate to the beauty of the character of those who lived there. But there was a serpent in that garden and so it became a wilderness.

Thus in the story of redemption we come to another garden, Gethsemane. "He went forth with his disciples across the Kidron valley, where there was a garden, which he and his disciples entered" (John 18:1 RSV). The garden of Eden was a scene of defeat: the garden of Gethsemane was a place of victory. There under the shadow of the olive trees, Jesus won the great victory of the spirit and planted the passion flower of resignation to the Father's will. This was the crowning point of his suffering. When he left the garden he had already won his triumph. Robertson Nicoll once preached a sermon entitled "Gethsemane, the Rosegarden of God," and took as his text the words in the Epistle to the Hebrews, "Without shedding of blood there is no remission of sins" (Hebrews 9:22). He stopped at the word "no." Without shedding of blood, he argues, there is nothing, no mighty achievement, no triumph. "No life will bring forth fruit to God if it is without its Gethsemane. Just as the blood of the Savior dropped in Gethsemane, and the ground blessed it, so the blood of the surrendered soul makes its Gethsemane a garden." It is a beautiful symbolism that as in a garden the first Adam lost his birthright, so in a garden the second Adam won it back. As John Henry Newman put it:

> O wisest love that flesh and blood
> Which did in Adam fail,
> Should strive afresh against the foe,
> Should strive and should prevail.

That is appropriate. But does this assertion of our text seem so? Our first thought, as we read these words, is one of disharmony. How unsuitable that amid a scene of exquisite loveliness the foulest deed ever committed should take place! How often we have noticed a similar disparity between our own heart and the appearance of external nature! When some great sorrow has darkened your days, and all that life seemed meant for fails, you awaken next morning to find the sunshine flooding your room as if nothing had happened. All the world is full of joy on this spring morning, but in your heart there is misery and gloom. Or it may be that your heart is full of joy and you see nothing but a frowning landscape and a weeping sky.

Nature seems unresponsive alike to your pain or pleasure.

We feel the same incongruity when we see this garden around the Cross and watch the flowers blooming gaily and filling the air with their fragrance, while the greatest tragedy of history is being enacted. But if our first thought is one of incongruity between the scenery and its scene, is not our second thought one of its essential harmony and fitness? And in this case, second thoughts are best. This may well be illustrated from the Greek legend of Hyacinthus. He and Apollo were playing quoits together, and Apollo threw his quoit high up in the air. Hyacinthus, excited by the game, ran forward to catch it as it fell. He missed it; and the quoit, bounding back from a stone which it struck, hit him on the forehead. He fell bleeding to the ground and though Apollo hastened to his aid, the wound was fatal. But when they removed his body they noticed that the blood which had flowed from his forehead was no longer blood. In its stead flowers sprang up of purple color and fragrant perfume. Ever since then, by the will of Apollo, the flower called hyacinth blooms again every spring. Thus he died on the hillsides of Greece, and in the place where he bled there were blossoms.

That is a striking parallel to the words of our text. The scene of the death of Christ was the scene of new splendors. Wherever the Cross has been planted in the soil of human life it has always made a garden of it. Jesus was mistaken by Mary on Easter morning for a gardener, and as Spurgeon says, there is a deep truth in this superficial error. Christ is the true gardener of human souls, and wherever the Cross has been uplifted there have bloomed around it the passion flowers of repentance, the roses of love, and the lilies of purity.

The planting of a Cross in the midst of a garden long ago

has been a true prophecy of all the ages. In the Christian life there is many a cross, but that is just the place where we may find the garden that God has planted around it. Life would be an intolerable burden were it not for its garden aspect. There were would be no flowers if the sun were always hidden behind dark clouds. God does not allow things to operate in that way. He never permits the cold, biting frosts of winter utterly to destroy the roots of plants and trees. But the price of fruitfulness is sacrifice. The very words "bless" and "blessed" are derived from the Anglo-Saxon word "blood." The word "blossom" is also derived from the same root. Blessing comes from blood. Wherever there is a cross there is a garden.

Think what a barren place the world would be if Christ had never hung on the Cross. Coulson Kernahan has a remarkable dream-allegory called "The Man of No Sorrows." An Eastern prophet arrives in London announcing that he is the new savior of the world. Sorrow and pain, he says, have no place in the universe and human society will never be saved until sorrow is discredited. The people eagerly accept this teaching, and tears and sorrow are banished. Years pass. All suffering is repressed with the result that the race gradually becomes selfish. Sympathy ceases to exist: the very word is deleted from the dictionary. No poets are born, for poets are the children of pain, who learn by suffering what they teach in song. Music and painting are no longer practiced, and the loss of these arts drives the people to despair. At last in their rage they turn on the man of no sorrows and drive him out, turning once again to the teaching of Jesus that he who suffers most has most to give.

Think what the world would have lost if Jesus had never died on Calvary. Milton would not have written *Paradise*

Regained. Tennyson would never have composed *In Memoriam*. Many of the poems of Browning, Whittier, and Lowell would have remained unwritten. The pictures of Velasquez and Raphael, Burne-Jones and Rossetti would have been lost to the world. Bach's Passion music and Handel's *Messiah* would never have been written. It is when you think along these lines and remember how these various ministries to the human mind—art, literature, and music— have redeemed the world from barrenness that you can see the application of our text to the Saviorhood of Christ.

There is a famous picture by G. F. Watts called *Love and Life*. Love is depicted as an angel, life as a naked woman. They are ascending together the rocky slopes of a mountain. Life is unprotected except by the wings of love. The hands of love are outstretched ready to help. If you look closely at the picture you will see that wherever life has placed her feet on the rocky slopes which she is climbing, sweet old-fashioned flowers have burst into bloom. Wherever the sharp stones have torn her feet, as she journeys over the mountain with love, the blood-drops have blossomed. Bloodshed blossoms into beauty on the road where life journeys with love.

Was this not true of the whole earthly life of our Lord? His was a pilgrimage along rugged steeps, but it was made in company with love. Read through the Gospels with that thought in your mind and notice the effects Christ produced during his public ministry. He always left a sense of sympathy with those who suffered. Men and women felt that he was afflicted in all their afflictions, that the hand of tragedy which had touched them had laid its hand upon his shoulder also. And to complete his identification with the sin and suffering of mankind he died upon the Cross, and in the place where he bled there were blossoms. As George Matheson puts it in his famous hymn:

> O Cross that liftest up my head,
> I dare not ask to fly from thee;
> I lay in dust life's glory dead,
> And from the ground there blossoms red
> Life that shall endless be.

Sorrow and pain and loss come to us all. Everything depends on our reaction to them. We may be bitter and resentful and rebellious. Or we may set our teeth and grimly bear our trials. But if we are wise, we shall turn our liabilities into assets. There is nothing that can possibly happen to us which need defeat us. Christ shows us his pierced hands marred for our sakes. Those hands are a witness to the wounds which sin has inflicted upon God. But they are also a triumphant proof of the victory which his love has achieved on the Cross. Whatever we may have to suffer is nothing compared with what Christ suffered on Calvary.

What are we going to make of Christ? This is the challenge of Good Friday. This is the choice forced upon us. There is no evading it. Calvary is inevitable. It is a narrow place, and there is no turning. God stands at the entrance, not like the angel with the flaming sword at the entrance to the Garden of Eden, but showing us his wounded hands and side. Why should we flee from him? Let us turn our footsteps again to the Cross of the Son of man and hear his words of peace. And then we will walk in the garden nearby, where the tomb lies empty and all the hymns of Easter are heralding the resurrection and life is bathed in glory—the glory of God who has passed through the darkness and shed on a world of sin and sorrow the light of a love which has fought and won.

EASTER DAY

X

The Gospel of the Resurrection

You seek Jesus of Nazareth, who was crucified. He has risen, he is not here; see the place where they laid him.

Mark 16:6 RSV

What is the characteristic word of the Christian religion? Suppose you were asked to single out one word to express the cardinal truth of the gospel, what word would you choose? I suggest it would have to be the word "resurrection." According to the Bible that is what Christianity essentially is, a religion of resurrection. The preachers of the early church never pointed men to the Cross without showing them the resurrection light breaking behind it. What gave their preaching such power was their testimony that this same Jesus was alive and present and at work in the world. Christ risen and living was for them the one dominating reality of life. Without the resurrection there would be no New Testament, no Sunday, no Christian church.

If you were to ask me what is the chief source of Christianity's power, my answer would be, not the life of Jesus, wonderful though that is; not the teaching of Jesus, precious though that is; not even the Cross; but the empty tomb. You cannot link Christ and Christianity except through the resurrection. Christianity hangs onto Christ not merely as to a person who lived and taught and died, but one who rose again from the dead and is alive forevermore. The first native Indian bishop, Dr. Azariah of Dornakal, when asked one day, "If you were in a village where they had never heard of Christ, what would you preach about?" answered without hesitation. "The resurrection." Christianity celebrates the crucifixion once a year, on Good Friday, but the resurrection is celebrated fifty-two times a year. For every Sunday is the day of the Lord, the day of resurrection. Christianity's symbol is not the dead figure of the crucifix, but Christ risen, trampling a broken Cross under his feet.

On Easter Sunday, 1960, Dr. W. E. Sangster, one of British Methodism's finest preachers, lay speechless and helpless. He wrote a message to his daughter, Margaret: "It is terrible to wake up on Easter morning and have no voice with which to shout, 'he is risen.' But it would be still more terrible to have a voice and not want to shout."

After the crucifixion there had not been time to render the last services to the body of Jesus. The Sabbath had intervened, and the women who wished to anoint the body had not been able to do so. Immediately the Sabbath was passed, as early as possible, they set out on their sad task. They were worried about one thing. Tombs had no doors. When the word "door" is mentioned it really means an opening. In front of the opening there was a groove, and in the groove a circular stone as big as a cart wheel, and the women knew that it was quite beyond their strength to move a stone like that. But when they reached the tomb, the stone had already been rolled away, and inside was the messenger who said: "Do not be amazed; you seek Jesus of Nazareth, who was crucified. He has risen, he is not here; see the place where they laid him."

THE GOSPEL OF THE RESURRECTION

One thing is certain—if Jesus had not risen from the dead, we should never have heard of him. Nothing else could have changed sad and despairing men and women into people radiant with joy and flaming with courage. The resurrection is the central fact of the Christian faith. Alice Meynell, in her poem *Christ in the Universe*, says that "our wayside planet . . . bears as its chief treasure one forsaken grave." At Easter time Christians all over the world go again to that forsaken grave and there renew their faith in the Savior's resurrection.

He is risen, and therefore, even in a world like this, so troubled and threatened, so full of griefs and graves, we may be assured of his presence with us and of his help in every time of need. Jesus is not a memory, but a Presence, someone whom we meet.

> Warm, sweet, tender, even yet
> A present help is he;
> And faith has still its Olivet,
> And love its Galilee.
>
> —J. G. Whittier

This is what Easter has meant in the hearts of multitudes of believers—that Jesus is alive, the same Jesus who once in Galilee was the friend of sinners, the comfort of the sad, man's comrade and helper. The Jesus who was with Paul in the wilds of Asia, with John on the isle of Patmos, with Peter in the Roman arena—this same Jesus still travels through the world in the greatness of his strength, mighty to save, still meets the troubled heart with the divine promise, "Lo, as I was with those others, so I will be with you." If sorrow should visit your heart or your home, you will not be left alone. "I will not leave you comfortless: I will come to you" (John 14:18). Whatever in this insecure world we may lose,

Christ will never leave us nor forsake us. He will always be ours. The death which could not hold our rising Lord will never be able to tear us from his grasp.

At the southernmost point of South Africa is a cape round which the storms are always raging. For a thousand years no one knew what lay beyond that cape, for no ship had ever returned to tell the tale. It was called the Cape of Storms. In the sixteenth century a Portuguese explorer, Vasco da Gama, successfully sailed around the cape and found beyond it a great calm sea and beyond that the shores of India. So the name of the cape was changed to the Cape of Good Hope. Until Christ rose from the dead, death had been the cape of storms on which the hopes of all mankind were wrecked and no one knew what lay beyond it. But now, in the light of Easter, it has become for all who believe in Christ, the cape of good hope, and we know that beyond it lies the shore of heaven.

Dietrich Bonhoeffer, the German theologian who was imprisoned during World War II and was executed on April 8, 1945, had conducted a service for his fellow prisoners just before they came to take him to his death, and this was his text: "Blessed be the God and Father of our Lord Jesus Christ! By his great mercy we have been born anew to a living hope through the resurrection of Jesus Christ from the dead" (I Peter 1:3 RSV). As he left with the guards he said to a British officer: "This is the end but for me the beginning of life." That is the authentic Christian attitude in the face of death.

The trouble with many of us is that we are living on the wrong side of Easter. We are back where the disciples were between Good Friday and the resurrection. We stand helpless before the evil that is in the world. We need to start living on the right side of Easter. God has spoken, and his last word about his children is not death but life. It is the gospel of the resurrection that holds the answer to this world's need. If it is false, there is no hope for humanity anywhere. If it is true, then all our dreams are true. As day follows night, each with its new troubles, its added perplexity, let us listen, and we will hear our Savior say, "Lo, I am with you always."

2. He is risen, and therefore, even in a world like this, we know that love is conqueror. Jesus believed in love, met the hatred of men only with love, and hatred seemed to triumph over him. He believed in God, ventured wholly upon God, and it seemed as though God had forsaken him. And if his story had ended at the Cross it would have seemed that this was a world where love was too weak a thing to live, a world where there was no God, or only a baffled and threatened God. But that is not the end of the story. Christ is risen, and in his resurrection love has triumphed and God has manifested his power.

Dr. Robert F. Horton tells a story of a woman who over a period of twenty years greatly influenced his life. One Christmas morning she gave him a present which she said was in two parts. One was a sketch of a garden: the other she would not disclose. A few days later she died suddenly, and in his grief he forgot the other half of the gift. But one morning in the spring he returned from a brief holiday to discover that his garden was a mass of crocus blooms. Unknown to him, his friend had planted them in the winter—they were the second part of her gift. He says that as he looked out on that mass of loveliness every flower seemed to be saying, "Love does not die". This is the meaning of Joseph's garden. Love does not, cannot, die. But it says more than that. The resurrection is not survival; it is victory.

If today it seems to us that love is too weak and powerless a thing to contend against the forces of hate and fear, let us remember how once those forces did their worst and were defeated. Love was crucified, but love rose again. Love can never be finally defeated. God will never allow those who face the world in Christ's way to be put to confusion. The power of God that broke the concentrated might of evil in the rising again of Jesus shall yet resurrect the world. Through his death and resurrection we may be more than conquerors, for in his love Christ shares with us the victory he has won.

Do you know the story of how the news of the battle of Waterloo came to London? It was brought by sailing ship to the south coast of England and then semaphored to the capital. One of the signalers was on the roof of Winchester Cathedral, and, having received the message, he semaphored to the next station the words "Wellington defeated" and had got no further when a fog closed in, and the semaphore could not be seen. When the message reached London it plunged the whole city into gloom. Then the fog lifted and the semaphore on the Cathedral could be seen again and this time was able to send the completed message: "Wellington defeated the enemy." And all the more glorious for the preceding gloom, the wonderful news spread across the land and caused rejoicing. The fact of Good Friday is part of a divine message to man. But it is only part; and not until the whole message is known, when the fact of Easter Day is added to it, will it stir us to thanksgiving.

3. He is risen, and therefore, even in a world like this, we know that some day Christ shall reign as King. "Jesus of Nazareth, king" they wrote in derision over the Cross. They put on him the purple robe of mockery and crowned him

with a crown of thorns. There was no one to do him reverence then, save a few humble friends; and even they doubted him. But on Easter Day we see this same Jesus, whom men despised and rejected, crowned with glory and honor. God took the Cross on which they nailed his Son and made of it a throne from which he should reign as king. Through the ages Christ has reigned from the tree, reigned in the hearts of those whom his love has conquered. Someday he will reign in the world's life, and the kingdoms of this world will become the kingdom of our Lord and of his Christ, and he shall reign forever and ever. At Easter we hail him as our heart's conquering Lord and the destined King of all the world.

Ibsen, the Norwegian dramatist, pictures the Emperor Julian, who cried, "Thou hast conquered, O pale Galilean," as going on to say: "Where is he now? What if he goes on and on, suffering and dying, conquering again and again from one world to the next?" In this troubled world, with its wars and rumors of wars, we see little sign of God's kingdom. But it is there, we may be sure, postponed perhaps, but not defeated. It is waiting to come in when men are ready to take God's way. It is the only kingdom that will finally stand. Other kingdoms and other policies may have supremacy for a time, but they will bring about their own destruction. "We have a kingdom that cannot be shaken."

Christ is risen, and therefore we can be assured of his presence and help in every time of need. Christ is risen, and therefore we know that love is conqueror. Christ is risen, and therefore we know that some day he shall reign on earth. This is the gospel of the resurrection, and it is good news indeed.

On the night before Easter Day, crowds of pilgrims gather

in the Church of the Holy Sepulchre in Jerusalem outside the closed doors of the cavern which is reputed to be the tomb in which Jesus lay. At midnight the sacred fire is kindled within the cavern, and the doors of the church are opened. The pilgrims press forward to receive from the hands of the priests candles that have been lighted from the holy fire. With these candles they light the lanterns they have brought and go out into the night.

So let us rekindle the lamps of faith and hope and love at the empty tomb of our Lord from the fire that burns so brightly there. Let us guard henceforth in our hearts that rekindled light that it may not again be put out. That light will guide us home, and it may be that some other pilgrim whose own light has gone out will rekindle his lamp from ours, as he learns from us to rejoice in the Easter fact that Christ is risen.

ASCENSION DAY

XI

Our Man in Heaven

As they were looking on, he was lifted up, and a cloud took him out of their sight.

Acts 1:9 RSV

There is a grave in a London cemetery which has a stone erected over it by a great preacher to the memory of a beloved wife. When he came to prepare the inscription he could not bring himself to write "Died." He chose the word "Ascended." When he himself passed over, those who were left remembered his chosen word and used it of him also: "Joseph Parker Born April 9, 1830, Ascended Nov. 28, 1902." That is how some souls are able to think who have seen the end of their faith. But they would not have been so sure of their own upward track if they had not seen their Lord go up before them.

There are some Christians who, when Ascensiontide comes round, feel themselves at their favorite point of the whole Christian year. Different minds will always be specially attracted to different parts of the story of the Savior. As we read the lives of God's saints, it seems as though one lives especially under the spell of the Incarnation, another under that of the Passion. There was one famous saint who professed a special devotion to the winding sheet and the sepulcher. But there are at least a few who, if they had the choice given them of building the tabernacle of their favorite contemplation at Bethlehem or at Nazareth or on Mount Tabor or at Calvary or on Olivet, would of all those places choose Olivet because from there they can see the most. From the Mount of Olives they can look up into the opened heavens and round upon the waiting world with its tasks, back upon a finished redemption and on into the wonder of the promised kingdom.

Once upon a time it was possible to take the story of the Ascension literally. The earth was flat: over it was "that inverted bowl they call the sky." As there was a Hades under men's feet, so there was a heaven over their heads. The old cosmogony has gone, and now that we know ourselves to be in a universe not in the least like that—a universe in motion, and our little world in motion as much as the rest of it—it may seem that such a word as "Ascension" is altogether out of date. Yet one of the most widespread thoughts is the conception of a plane of being higher than the world in which we live. We still speak of high ideals and lofty aims, and of some ambitions as low and of Heaven as the high and holy place. We know that the earth revolves around the sun; yet we continue to speak of sunsets and sunrises, and our language deceives no one.

"Ascension" is a symbolic word: "higher plane" is a symbolic phrase: any word we can use is but a symbol and a picture. But Christians will cling to the word they know and love. Jesus ascended, not into any land of promise to be found over our heads, but into higher levels of being than this earthly existence provides, where God himself is the light and where no clouds obscure his glory. From those levels Christ came, to those levels he belonged, into those he went; there he still lives and reigns and loves. He spoke of himself as having come "from above," "from the Father," or as one apostle tenderly adds, "from the bosom of the Father." As his mission on earth came to an end, Jesus often dwelt on the thought that he was going to the Father. From the Father, to the Father—the one thought completes the other. We do not get all the light and comfort that wait for us in the story of Jesus if we merely say of him what Tennyson said of King Arthur, "From the great deep to the great deep he goes." Christ filled the deeps with glory when he wrote across them, "From the Father—to the Father."

The first truth that is revealed in the Ascension of our Lord is that the life of the world to come is an embodied life. Christianity knows nothing of the immortality of the soul apart from the body. It knows nothing of disembodied spirits. Recent biology and psychology have emhasized the concept of the body-mind as a "going concern." This is precisely the Christian idea of personality here and hereafter. The resurrection of the body is a Christian doctrine enshrined in the New Testament record.

This must not be confused with the resurrection of the material flesh. Here Paul is our best guide. "It is sown a physical body; it is raised a spiritual body" (I Corinthians 15:44 RSV). The resurrection body of Christ was not subject to the limitations of physical life. His spirit was in complete control. It is the same body that hung upon the Cross, recognizable for his loved ones, but it is spiritualized. He can enter a room when the door is shut: he can manifest himself and then be hidden from their eyes; and at last he can be parted from them and be carried up into heaven.

The Ascension was the last of a series of appearances and disappearances, and it stands for his returning to the eternal realm from which he came. The life of heaven, the life of the spiritual realm, is an embodied life, continuing the life of personal identity we have known on earth. The resurrection life is not that of gods and angels, but of human beings. The Ascension stands for the truth: "I believe in the resurrection of the body"—that is, the preserving of personal identity, the soul clothed in a form which can be recognized and which maintains those precious characteristics which make life dear to us. Paul put it best: "It is sown in dishonor, it is raised in glory. It is sown in weakness, it is raised in power " (I Corinthians 15:43). Our Lord ascended and went on to prepare a place for his disciples, and on the authority of his word and of his Ascension, those who are forever with the Lord shall be clothed with the glory of a spiritual body in the heaven of his presence.

The second truth revealed in the Ascension of our Lord is that the Incarnation not only brought God to earth, but carried man to heaven. Only the picture language of a throne in the heavens can tell of the wonder of the Ascension. The place of Christ at the right hand of God is affirmed in every part of the New Testament. Charles Wesley, in one of his Ascension hymns, expresses this truth in vivid language.

> See! He lifts his hands above;
> See! He shows the prints of love;
> Hark! His gracious lips bestow
> Blessings on his Church below.

The form men knew and loved—the same hands, the same lips—bless from high heaven. This is pictorial and poetic, for in no other way can such truth be communicated. There is a man in heaven. Jesus ascended as a human being. The word of instruction uttered to the disciples on the Mount of

Olives was, "This Jesus, who was taken up from you into heaven, will come in the same way as you saw him go into heaven" (Acts 1:11 RSV). Jesus . . . in the same way, that is, a human being, abides and will abide to the end, akin to us men.

We see Jesus glorified but still the same Jesus. Jean Ingelow asks:

> And didst thou take to heaven a human brow?
> Dost plead with man's voice by the marvelous sea?
> Art thou his kinsman now?

Yes, he is. We have an ally and a director in the heavenly places. As the writer to the Hebrews put it: "He ever liveth to make intercession for [us]" (Hebrews 7:25). The Son of man in heaven interprets our groanings that cannot be uttered, our inarticulate penitence, aspiration, and prayer. He appears before the face of God for us. He does this because he is the Son of man.

> He hath raised our human nature
> In the clouds to God's right hand.

He ceaselessly strives on our behalf, because he is the same yesterday, today, and forever. As Charles Wesley says:

> He pleads his passion on the tree,
> He shows himself to God for me.

The third truth which is revealed in the Ascension of our Lord is that we worship not only a crucified Savior but our ascended and glorified Lord. The Cross is the symbol of redeeming love; the Ascension is the sign of triumphant power. "On his head were many crowns" (Revelation 19:12). The crucified is King. "The head that once was crowned with thorns is crowned with glory now." The Ascension is the coronation of Christ. He sits upon the throne of God and turns the wrath of man to his praise. He is doing this now. He does it whether men recognize his kingship or not, while evil, at his permission, stalks the earth; when men faint for fear and expectation of the things that are coming on the earth; when the church is cold and divided in counsel, and we are worldly and proud. "We do not yet see everything in subjection to him. But we see Jesus, who for a little while was made lower than the angels, crowned with glory and honor" (Hebrews 2:8-9 RSV).

Jesus ascended in order to reign. As Paul put it: "He must reign until he has put all his enemies under his feet" (I Corinthians 15:25 RSV). "He was raised . . . far above all rule and authority and power and dominion, . . . not only in this age but also in that which is to come" (Ephesians 1:21 RSV). Jesus had to ascend into heaven to begin his universal rule. "The suffering, dying Jesus is the Christ upon the throne." It is his world. All authority has been given to him. Exult this Ascensiontide as you see him take the throne.

This world does not look as though it belongs to Jesus. Murder, lust, greed, selfishness, pride, and jealousy are spread wide across it; and the battle between good and evil seems as sharp as it ever was. It seems at times as though the good is losing ground, as though truth were forever on the scaffold and wrong were forever on the throne, as James Russell Lowell put it. But the real victory is already won. For Christ overcame the world at Calvary. It is his world now. Christ is on the throne. New faith and courage and hope will be born in our hearts if that truth is grasped and believed.

The Ascension of Jesus into heaven is also his ascension

to his throne in human hearts. John Wesley once said, "If we could bring all our preachers to insist that Christ not only died *for* us but Christ must reign *in* us, we should shake the trembling gates of hell." Jesus reigns forever on the throne of God. It depends upon you how soon his kingdom comes, on your abdication of the throne of your life in his favor. For the throne of God is in the human heart. Can I hope that Christ will conquer the world if he has not conquered my heart? Can he have his way with society if I give him no chance to have his way with me? Let Christ dictate your every action and attitude and make him King in your life. He will not wrest the throne from you. He waits for you to offer it to him.

Have you recognized and yielded to such complete lordship as Christ deserves and demands? Let us be honest about it. We are not ready to let go of ourselves and let this Christ of many crowns walk into every nook and cranny of our lives and claim everything for himself. It may be a bad temper. It may be an undisciplined, pleasure-loving mind. It may be a smoldering resentment. It may be a fear of unpopularity. Whatever it is that holds us back from making Christ King of our lives, let us renounce it. Let us hand over all the keys of control to our risen and ascended Lord and crown him Lord of all.

PENTECOST

XII

Three Responses to Pentecost

All were amazed and perplexed, saying to one another, "What does this mean?" But others mocking said, "They are filled with new wine."
                                                        Acts 2:12-13 RSV
This is what was spoken by the prophet Joel: . . .
                                                        Acts 2:16

There are three great days in the year for the Christian—Christmas, Easter, and Pentecost. We know what Christmas is, the birthday of Jesus. We know what that birth has meant to the world. Moreover, we are familiar with the fact of birth, and we all celebrate birthdays in our own families. We know what Easter is, the day on which Jesus was raised from the dead. We do not understand so clearly what that means because resurrection is a little further beyond the range of our ordinary experience than the fact of birth. But we love Easter because it speaks to something deep within us. But Pentecost—what in the world is that? It was originally the name of a Jewish festival held fifty days after the Sabbath that followed Passover. To Christians it is the day which commemorates the descent of the Holy Spirit upon the apostles.

The events that took place on the day of Pentecost, as recorded in the second chapter of Acts, are what a few years

THREE RESPONSES TO PENTECOST

ago came to be called a "happening"—an event that is unexpected, unorganized, unplanned, yet vivid and exciting. The followers of Jesus were gathered in an upper room, and all of a sudden there rushed through the room a wind which almost blew the walls down; and then flames of fire came and lighted on the foreheads of all the people, burning no one but inducing them to speak in an amazing way so that everybody understood them, whether they spoke the same language or not. This remarkable happening called forth from those who observed it three revealing responses. Pentecost does so still. Let us examine these responses.

The first is *the response of bewilderment*. "All were amazed and perplexed, saying to one another, 'What does this mean?'" The New Testament account is couched in a language and imagery which are quite foreign to the twentieth century. The stage setting of the drama in an upper room in old Jerusalem is eerie. A whistling tornado is followed by the crackle of forked lightning, which scatters the men from their protected seclusion and hurls them into the open air to begin a world mission. It has well been described as the blast-off of the church into a new age.

Dr. Norman Maclean in his autobiography, *Years of Fulfilment*, tells a story of an examination in the Colinton Parish School. One teacher had taught a class to repeat the Apostles' Creed clause by clause, each pupil having his own clause. As the recitation began in the presence of the inspector, the first boy said, "I believe in God the Father Almighty, maker of heaven and earth." The second boy said, "I believe in Jesus Christ his only Son our Lord." So the recitation went on to the boy who said, "He ascended into heaven and sitteth on the right hand of God the Father Almighty: from thence he shall come to judge the quick and the dead." Then there fell a silence, which was finally broken by the next boy, who said to the inspector, "Please, sir, the boy who believes in the Holy Ghost is absent today." "Lots of people are absent when it come to that clause," is Dr. Maclean's comment.

The teaching concerning the Holy Spirit is the most vague and uncertain thing in the life of the church. Arthur Hird once described it as "the undiscovered country of Christianity, the dark continent of the Christian life, the land where our spiritual resources lie but lie undeveloped." Many Christians are bewildered, saying, what does this mean? It has been rightly said that if we try to understand all about the Holy Spirit we will lose our minds, but if we try to live without him we will lose our souls. The Holy Spirit is the life of God in the soul of man, not so much God above men, or God alongside men, as God inside them. "Christmas and Easter happened to Jesus Christ. Pentecost, to be real for you, must happen to you," said Stanley Jones. Pentecost is the greatest of all the Christian festivals if only we understood it aright. It completes Christmas and Easter by adding meaning to them. Easter would have no meaning apart from Christmas: what we rejoice in at Easter is that the same Jesus who was born and grew to manhood, who taught and healed in Palestine, who was known and loved by his disciples, who gave his life for them on the Cross, is still alive. In an even deeper sense, Christmas and Easter without Pentecost would be robbed of their fulness. At Pentecost the disciples first realized that Jesus was not only risen from the dead but was alive and active here and now. They had believed in him before Pentecost, but when the Holy Spirit came upon them, they were transformed. They were bold and fearless where before they had been cowardly and fearful. They knew then that God was with them still, as near to them as Christ himself ever was. So they went to their work with his companionship. They laid their plans under his guidance. They accomplished their tasks by his help.

A second response to the happening of Pentecost is *the response of disparagement*. "Others mocking said, 'They are filled with new wine.' " These critics standing on the edge of the crowd saw all that took place. They noted the fierce, extravagant excitement. They heard the wild, confused babbling. They observed the unbounded enthusiasm and said, "These men are drunk." So they were, but not because they were filled with wine but because they were filled with the Spirit.

What signs of drunkenness are to be seen in these Spirit-filled people? First, they have loosened tongues. One of the early and sure signs of intoxication is that people start talking freely. It was so here. These disciples, who a few hours earlier had been almost afraid of their own shadows and certainly afraid to speak aloud of their faith, now were declaring boldly the wonderful works of God. There was also the added wonder that people of different nationalities heard them in their own tongues. There is no surer sign today that we lack the power of God's Spirit than as Christians we are so tongue-tied. When the Holy Spirit came upon these people they simply could not keep their faith to themselves. Why are we so reticent about ours? There is something wrong with the person who has good news and does not spread it. Yet we have the greatest good news in the world, news concerning the salvation of God in Christ, and we are not making it known.

I know the difficulty. There are things too sacred to be shouted from the housetops. The glib parading of our innermost experience is distasteful. But that is not what

Peter did on the day of Pentecost. He did not reveal the remorse in his heart after his denial of Jesus, nor did he speak of his subsequent restoration. He said nothing about his own experience. But he did tell the people the good news that God had sent his Son to be the Savior of the world and that that Son, rejected of men, was now exalted to the right hand of God, and that belief in him would bring forgiveness. This is a day of good tidings, and to our shame we hold our peace. But the intoxication of God's Spirit can banish our inhibitions and loosen our tongues.

A second feature which these Spirit-filled people had in common with the intoxicated was their sense of being on good terms with everything and everybody. To the intoxicated man everything in the garden is lovely. He looks at the world through rosy spectacles. These Spirit-filled people did the same but for very different reasons. They were realists. They knew what was coming their way, but it did not seem to worry them. John, an old man in his eighties, is banished to the isle of Patmos. There he begins to see visions and to dream dreams. Stephen is being stoned to death, but his face is lit with the light of God. These men were drunk with the intoxication of God, filled with a spirit that took away all anxiety and fear.

The third feature which points to intoxication is their hilarity, their irrepressible joy. Christianity is indeed a divine intoxication. When it is real, it is a ferment in the heart. Jesus comes into a man's life with a rush, shaking him from his sin, changing all his values, so that his whole world is turned upside down. These disciples at Pentecost were crying out in an extravagant gladness which they could hardly understand. We read that they were praising the wonderful works of God. People do all sorts of foolish things when they are happy. They seem almost to walk on air. They burst into little snatches of song at the most awkward moments. Think of the joy of a sinner's soul finding God. It is not a remarkable thing that redeemed people should sing aloud: it is a remarkable thing that they should not. When one thinks of the love of God for people like us, the fullness and sweep of his forgiveness, our calling as children of God into eternal life with Christ—why, there is something wrong with us that we can take it so calmly! At least, in those early days when God's love in the Holy Spirit was revealed to the disciples, they were carried off their feet in amazed joy. What has happened to the joy which characterized so much worship in the past? A minister once told his congregation that if any one watched them coming into church he would think they were on their way to the dentist, and if the same person watched them coming out he would be sure that they had been.

The third response to the happening at Pentecost was *the response of discernment*. Peter, in the sermon he delivered to the crowd, said, "This is what was spoken by the prophet Joel: And in the last days it shall be, God declares, that I will pour out my spirit upon all flesh." Pentecost was something which the Lord did for them, and not something which they did for themselves. Whatever the sound as of the rushing of a mighty wind and the tongues of fire may mean, at least it means that there was something which came down from God. As Peter said, "God has poured out this which you see and hear." Nor was it something which merely happened once and has never been repeated. When you read the story of what happened to Saul of Tarsus on the Damascus road, or of what happened to Martin Luther as he toiled on his knees up the Sancta Scala in Rome, or of what happened to John Wesley in the meetinghouse on Aldersgate Street, what can you say but this, "God has poured out this which you see and hear"? What can you do but recall, as Peter did, the prophecy of Joel, and say, "This is that"?

The Holy Spirit is the power of Jesus active in the world. After Pentecost the disciples knew their Master's presence as an inward power: instead of his physical company they enjoyed his spiritual fellowship. Jesus was actually with them to save them and to equip them for all they had to do. Pentecost is the day on which the Spirit of Jesus came back and took hold of his followers and banded them into a closely knit community of the faith which we call the church and sent them out to continue his ministry in the world.

If it were not for Pentecost we would not be in church. We would have no gospel, no sacraments, no tradition, no fellowship. We would be on our own. We would not be here with one accord in one place, meeting together in the spirit of Jesus. When Toscanini retired and went back to Europe, he left his faithful musicians of the Symphony of the Air without a conductor. But they went on as though he were still their conductor. That shows us how a man's spirit can inspire others even when the man himself is not there. Our Conductor is not visibly present, but when we meet together we know that his Spirit is in our midst. He can still draw from us music that by ourselves we could never hope to make. He can do things with our imperfect instruments that will fit them for the important part they must play in the grand symphony of the world. If today we were to open our lives to Christ and allow his Spirit to possess us, a new Pentecost would come into our world.

TRINITY SUNDAY

XIII

God Speaks in Many Voices

In many and various ways God spoke of old to our fathers by the prophets; but in these last days he has spoken to us by a Son.
Hebrews 1:1-2 RSV

In the Bible we find a confidence that God speaks and a certainty that he speaks in many voices. The claim is made that God speaks through oracles, dreams, thunder, earthquakes, drought, famine, plague, and disaster. He spoke through the voices of angels, prophets, priests, and psalmists. He was heard in the burning bush, on the mountaintop, and in the caves. God's will for the world always found tongue and voice. His word was heard not as a sound in the ear but as a fact that had to be faced, and a deed that demanded to be done. Genesis puts it beautifully. When God said, "Let there be light," there was light. Light was the word of God, an act of God engaged in the work of creation.

When the sacred writings were gathered into one book, they were called "the Word of God." These writings were believed to contain his Word for all time. Scholars have studied them ceaselessly to discover the hidden meanings, the deeper truths believed to be there, like a rich vein of ore waiting to be mined. Long before the Christian era began, devout Jews treasured this Word of God and made it the law of life. They believed it contained a clue to God's purpose for them and his promise to be their God.

This was the star under which the Christian faith was born and brought to maturity. But with this tremendous difference—Christ was God's Word to man, his final and ultimate Word, based upon but superseding all other words. Thus in the New Testament we find the claim that while God has not left himself without a witness, anywhere, while he has spoken in many and various ways to our fathers by the prophets, in these last days he has spoken to us by a Son. Under the guidance of this faith, the early Christians put their own experiences into the New Testament which, together with the Old, became the Word of God for the Christian tradition.

I mention this not to make the point that God has spoken through many voices to our fathers before us but rather to make this one: God speaks through many voices to us today, even as he spoke to them. Hartley Coleridge, an English poet of the early nineteenth century, makes this point in these beautiful lines addressed to a young girl.

> In holy books we read how God hath spoken
> To holy men in many different ways.
> But hath the present world no sign or token?
> Is God quite silent in these latter days?
> O think it not, sweet maid: God comes to us
> With every day, with every star that rises,
> Believe that every bird that sings
> And every flower that stars the elastic sod,
> And every thought that happy summer brings,
> To thy pure spirit is a word of God.

The basic doctrines of the Christian faith derive from our experiences as well as from those of biblical times and events. The purpose of doctrine is not just to explain what our fathers believed the truth to be but to explain it in such a way that we shall discover and understand that truth in our own experience.

Let me illustrate this by reference to one of the basic doctrines in Christian thought—the Trinity. Trinity Sunday is the one Sunday in the Christian calendar dedicated simply to God, not to his mighty acts in history nor to any specific event in his incarnate life on earth in the person of Jesus Christ nor to the the workings of his Spirit in the church and the world, but simply to him—Father, Son, and Holy Spirit, one God. In the two ancient creeds of the church, the Apostles' and the Nicene, we say that we believe in God the Father Almighty, and in Jesus Christ, and in the Holy Spirit. "God in three Persons, blessed Trinity," we sing. After the responsive reading we sing, "Glory be to the Father, and to the Son, and to the Holy Spirit." The service of worship ends with the words, "May the blessing of God Almighty, the Father, the Son, and the Holy Spirit be with you always."

Thus we sing, thus we pray, but why? Why did our fathers come up with the doctrine of the Trinity, and why has it been so jealously guarded ever since? Christians cherish this doctrine because it is the most adequate interpretation we have of the ways in which we encounter the power and the will of God in life. God speaks to us not in one voice but in many, not in one way only but in several. God the Father is heard in creation, God the Son is heard in Jesus Christ; God the Holy Spirit is heard in the continuing guidance of God in life.

1. God speaks to us as creator of the universe. This is the

God of whom we speak when we say, "I believe in God the Father Almighty, maker of heaven and earth." No matter how intricate and vast the universe may be, God is its master. There is the kind of order in the universe which speaks of design, purpose, and mind. Thanks to the discoveries of the various sciences we know that we live in a cosmos, not a chaos. Science reveals a fundamental orderliness that stretches from atom to galaxy, from amoeba to man. As Albert Einstein said: "Certain it is that a conviction, akin to religious feeling, of the rationality and intelligibility of the world, lies behind all scientific work of a higher order."

To the conception of God as Creator found in Genesis, the Bible adds its own deeper interpretation, in the words of prophets and psalmists who think of the creative work of God in terms of their distinctive faith. When the writer of the forty-fifth chapter of Isaiah speaks about God's care for men and how he plans for their future, his faith is in one whose purposes go back to the creation itself, when God made the world a fit place for them to dwell in. "I form light and create darkness. . . . I made the earth, and created man upon it; it was my hands that stretched out the heavens, and I commanded all their host" (Isaiah 45:7, 12 RSV). Creation has not just been a physical process but there has been in it a purpose of righteousness. The New Testament links the fulfillment of this purpose also with the first creative act. "Worthy art thou, our Lord and God, to receive glory and honor and power, for thou didst create all things, and by thy will they existed and were created" (Revelation 4:11 RSV).

We believe that we hear the voice of God not only on the level of basic order in the world but also in the life processes themselves, calling life into being over a long period of growth and development. The climax of creation is the emergence of a being who can think God's thoughts after him, who is made in the image of God. We hear the voice of God speaking to us as Father in creation, as the one in whom we live and move and have our being. He is the God of infinite wisdom, love, and power whose will is always for the good of man. He is the Father who creates and nurtures, loves and guides his own.

2. It is the testimony of our fathers that, while they heard God's voice in other ways, they heard it with unequaled clarity and power in Jesus Christ. The word they heard was one of love and redeeming grace for all mankind. This is what makes the Christian religion different from all others. Other religions hear the Word of God in creation. There is no argument among us on this score. The real difference is whether or not we hear in Jesus Christ a word that reveals the very heart of God. In him we believe that we hear a unique word of God, of his love, purpose, and will. "He who has seen me has seen the Father" (John 14:9 RSV). "I and the Father are one" (John 10:30 RSV). That is Christ's own testimony. This is the great truth Paul had in mind when he wrote, "It is the God who said, 'Let light shine out of darkness,' who has shone in our hearts to give the light of the knowledge of the glory of God in the face of Christ" (II Corinthians 4, 6 RSV). The Apostle was telling the Corinthians in his day the same thing that E. Stanley Jones tells us in our day. "Look at Jesus and you will see exactly who God is."

The Nicene Creed declares that Jesus is "God of God, light of light, very God of very God, of one substance with the Father." When we read in the Gospels of Christ's compassion for the poor and the sick and the outcast, we know that this is exactly the way God acts. When we see Jesus suffering and dying on the Cross we know that this is the way God identifies himself with man in his agony on earth. On Easter morning when we sing, "He lives, He lives, Christ Jesus lives today," we know that we worship a living God who has conquered death and sin for our sakes so that one day we may live with him forever.

3. The doctrine of the Trinity says further that we hear the voice of God through the Holy Spirit. When the early Christians worked together or met in the evening for their meal or worshiped together, they believed that God was with them, "closer than breathing, nearer than hands or feet." They found that when they were brought up on trial before the magistrates they had no need to worry about it. God was with them and would put the words in their mouths that they were supposed to say. As they sought to live in Christ they discovered that Christ lived in them.

As we study the various experiences in New Testament times that bear witness to the Holy Spirit they suggest that he meant certain concrete things to the early Christians. The Holy Spirit meant power, the power of God which made courageous men out of cowards, which enabled Peter to say to the authorities, "We must obey God rather than men" (Acts 5:29 RSV). Empowered by this Spirit, the actual presence of God in his own life, Luther was able to face the entrenched powers of his day and say, "Here stand I; God helping me, I can do no other." It was the presence and urging of the Holy Spirit that caused John Wesley to face the taunt that he was a priest without a parish and to answer, "The world is my parish." The Nicene Creed refers to the Holy Spirit as "the Lord, the giver of life." When Cardinal Mindszenty was finally allowed to leave Hungary after twenty-two years as a political hostage, someone commented that he might as well have been dead for all those years. The Cardinal replied: "I would have died long ago if it had not been for God's Spirit sustaining me." Iron curtains and ideological walls are not strong enough to overcome the life-giving power of the Holy Spirit.

A second quality that the early Christians found in the company of the Holy Spirit was truth—the truth of God's will for man, of his love of man, of his presence in life and history. This explains the confidence with which they went about their world as witnesses to the Christian faith. Jesus had said to the Twelve as he sent them out on a mission, "When they deliver you up, do not be anxious how you are to speak or what you are to say; for what you are to say will be given you in that hour; for it is not you who speak but the Spirit of your Father speaking through you" (Matthew 10:19-20 RSV).

The experience of a love that would not let them go was another quality that found its way into the Christian conception of the Holy Spirit. Apart from the conviction that God spoke through the word of love, there is no adequate explanation of the life and teaching of our Lord. These make sense only on the assumption that God so loved the world that he gave his only begotten Son. The notion that love is power, the power of God, explains as nothing else can the amazing growth of the Christian fellowship through the centuries. The love that came through the Holy Spirit was the divine helper of all who sought to live as sons of God. The Holy Spirit is seeking to inform and direct the thought and life of those who are in the church.

In Jesus Christ we have come to know God as Father and Creator, the maker of our mortal bodies, the Father of our immortal souls, the giver of every good and perfect gift. In Jesus Christ we have come to know God as Son, the revealer of God, the redeemer and Savior of mankind. In Jesus Christ we have come to know God as the Holy Spirit, the

Counselor, the guide, the teacher who leads us into all truth. To know God thus is to have a rock on which faith can rest, certain that it never can be moved. Nothing short of this God in three Persons does justice to the experience of the early Christians. When they developed the doctrine of the Trinity they were interpreting their experience under the guidance of the Spirit. God the Father for us, eternally; God the Son with us in grace, historically but also eternally; God the Holy Spirit in us, experientially, historically, and eternally. Nothing less than such a faith does justice to the New Testament.

Horace Bushnell, in the early years before he became a famous preacher, was a tutor at Yale. Brilliant, restless, religiously perplexed, he came at last to spiritual assurance through a surrender to Christ. Later he confessed to his fellow tutors: "When the preacher touches the Trinity and when logic shatters it all to pieces, I am all at the four winds. But I am glad I have a heart as well as a head. My heart wants the Father; my heart wants the Son; my heart wants the Holy Spirit and one just as much as the other. My heart says the Bible has a Trinity for me and I mean to hold by my heart." The Trinity is a doctrine which is on the one hand intellectually balanced and complete, and on the other hand close to actual reality and to the needs of the heart. It can all be summed up in these lines:

> The whole round world is not enough to fill
> The heart's three corners, but it craveth still.
> Only the Trinity that made it can
> Suffice the vast-triangled heart of man.
> —Christopher Hervey

ALL SAINTS' DAY

XIV

The Communion of Saints

We are surrounded by so great a cloud of witnesses.

Hebrews 12:1 RSV

November 1 is All Saints' Day. It is the day set apart to underscore our belief in the communion of saints. This term has two meanings. It speaks of the unity by which all Christians on earth are bound to one another in Christ. It also speaks of the unity that prevails between the church on earth and the church in heaven. It is a festival which John Wesley in his Journal twice confesses that he dearly loves. It did not matter to him on what day of the week it came. He observed it with triumphant joy. "On this day in particular," he writes, "I find the truth of the words":

> The Church triumphant in Thy love
> Their mighty joys we know.
> They sing the Lamb in hymns above,
> And we in hymns below.
> —Charles Wesley

This day is dedicated to the memory of all those who counted not their lives dear unto themselves, who fought the good fight, who kept the faith, finished their course, and have entered into the joy of their Lord. The church on this day recalls the obscure and unknown faithful, all the holy and humble men of heart, the saints whom the world never knew but who are known to God, whose names are written in the Lamb's book of life.

Thirteen hundred years ago the church gathered from their burial place in the Catacombs of Rome the remains of nameless Christians who, in the days of persecution, had won the martyr's crown. In honor of these faithful ones Pope Boniface IV instituted the festival of All Saints. As time passed, this festival was celebrated in memory, not only of those who died in the arena, but of all the saints who in any age or country have lived and died for Christ.

The doctrine of the communion of saints has been somewhat neglected by certain sections of the Christian church. The abuse to which it has given rise may help to explain the scant attention it has received. There is the practice of the invocation of the saints. They have been invoked for all kinds of trivial purposes. While there is no reason why we should not, if we desire, invoke the aid of the saints, it is beyond dispute that such invocation has often led to worship and adoration. It is right that we should suspect any practice that discourages man's direct approach to God or that leads to the worship of the creature rather than the Creator. But we need to be reminded that an age that idolizes baseball players, movie stars, and beauty queens should be chary of criticizing those whose tastes lie elsewhere. When a devout soul on earth promises me his or her prayer, I accept that service as the greatest gift that can be made. How much greater the service when, as saints in light, they pray. By faith we join our hands with those who have gone before us.

Prayers for the dead are associated with this doctrine. This practice has been a fruitful source of superstition in the

THE COMMUNION OF SAINTS

history of the church. Nevertheless it cannot be ruled out on Christian grounds. It is difficult for us to imagine the needs of those who have passed into another life, but it is surely open for us to pray that they may grow in grace and in the knowledge of the love of God. The dead, it is true, are in the hands of God, but are not the living also? The fact of death need not interrupt our intercessions. Why should we not pray for those of our number who have gone before and especially for those whom we have known and loved, for whom we often prayed when they were with us in the flesh? Why should we hesitate to believe that those who in their life on earth knew and loved us still hold us in memory and help us by their prayers to God?

In the eleventh chapter of Hebrews, following the roll call of the heroes of the faith in Old Testament times, the writer says: "All these, though well attested by their faith, did not receive what was promised, since God had foreseen something better for us, that apart from us they should not be made perfect" (Hebrews 11:39-40 RSV). They have run their leg of the relay race, but they have not moved on from the track to the quiet and privacy of the locker room. Rather, they surround us like a great cloud of witnesses because they have a stake in seeing and knowing that we further the work in which they lived and died.

When we speak of the saints we instinctively think of heaven and the church triumphant, of those whose warfare is over and who now share the glory of the Lord. But the term "saints" in the New Testament is not confined to the glorified. To the apostle Paul every Christian was a saint. He addresses his first letter to the Christians in Corinth thus: "To the church of God which is at Corinth, to those sanctified in Christ Jesus, called to be saints" (I Corinthians 1:2 RSV). The members of that church were far from perfect, but as Dr. Alan Richardson reminds us, "the saint of the New Testament is not a perfected being, but a forgiven sinner." A saint is one who is consecrated to God, dedicated, set apart to his will. Everyone who lives for Christ and in whom Christ lives is a saint in the New Testament sense of the term. What the doctrine of the communion of saints asserts is that between all who love our Lord there is a gracious and beautiful fellowship.

What kind of communion of saints does the New Testament contemplate? No one can read the Gospels without feeling that our Lord looked for unity to prevail among his followers. But it was not external unity of organization he had in mind. "There shall be one flock, one shepherd" (John 10:16 RSV). The unity is found not in the fact that the sheep are all gathered within the same four walls but that they are all under the loving care of the one shepherd. Paul says: "We who are many are one body, for we all partake of the one bread" (I Corinthians 10:17 RSV). He is speaking of the bread at the Lord's table. The taking of that bread, he says, is a communion of the body of Christ; that is to say, spiritually we receive into our souls the very life of Christ when we eat that bread in faith. That is what makes us all one body—not that we belong to the same visible organization but that we all eat of the same bread and share in the same divine life. The real ground of communion is Christ; and because of that, in spite of the sects and division in the church, we can say in the words of the Apostles' Creed, "I believe in the communion of saints."

I believe in it as a fact. We build our ecclesiastical party walls high and strong; but no party walls, however high, can keep kindred spirits apart. There is freemasonry of Christian souls. The Lord's people recognize one another. In the hymnal we have a concrete illustration of the

THE COMMUNION OF SAINTS

communion of saints. Catholic and Protestant, Trinitarian and Unitarian, Quaker and Methodist, all meet in the pages of the hymnal. Nothing can hinder that holy fellowship or destroy it. We are not strangers but fellow citizens of the household of God. Let us believe in the communion of saints and cultivate it. Let us do what we can to promote actual and visible fellowship through the ecumenical movement.

> Blest be the tie that binds
> Our hearts in Christian love:
> The fellowship of kindred minds
> Is like to that above.

I believe in the communion of saints not only as a fact but as a force. It is a great inspiration and power. The Christian life is a social life. It is meant to be lived in fellowship with other men and women of the like faith. That is why the writer of Hebrews bids us not to forsake the assembling of ourselves together. We are enjoying the communion of saints when we meet together for worship every Sunday. We enjoy it in a still deeper and more intimate fashion when we meet around the table of the Lord. The whole atmosphere of public worship would be altered if we did but realize that the worshipers are drawn from heaven and earth. We tend to imagine that the worshipers are confined to the visible congregation. Hence we are often dismayed to find the number so small. But the smallest congregation is not as small as it appears to be, and the largest congregation seems small compared with the heavenly host which shares our worship.

Are we not inspired to more heroic endeavor when we recall that we are running the race in the presence of a great cloud of witnesses who watch over us with loving care?

They belong to us as we belong to them. They rejoice over our victories and uphold us by their prayers in the time of temptation. The church of Christ in heaven and on earth is one and indivisible. It is all one blessed and glorious body. Dull must he be of soul who does not thrill to those triumphant words in the Communion service which say: "Therefore with angels and archangels and with all the company of heaven, we laud and magnify thy glorious name."

To realize that we are members of this vast host, to enter into the communion of saints, is to be lifted up above all doubts and fears. There is inspiration to fidelity and steadfastness in the thought of those spiritual presences with whom we are one in Christ. What a thrilling thing ordinary churchgoing might become if we always kept the communion of saints in mind. It would save us from defeatism. How often our attitude seems to say: "We Christians are a pitiful minority. Here is a congregation gathered in the house of God in the name of Christ, but for everyone of us here are there not hundreds of men and women for whom Christ means nothing?" When that mood gets hold of us we would do well to pause and remember the mighty, invisible host with whom we hold high fellowship every time we gather in God's house, the great multitude whom no man can number, of all nations and kindreds and people and tongues standing before the throne and before the Lamb, with the perfect praise of heaven upon their lips. When we are inclined to attach small importance to our church and congregation and to our own place in the Christian community, let us think ourselves anew into the full width and sweep and grandeur of the heritage that is ours.

Later on in this chapter of Hebrews the writer describes

THE COMMUNION OF SAINTS

what happens when we come together for worship. "You have come to Mount Zion and to the city of the living God, the heavenly Jerusalem, and to innumerable angels in festal gathering, and to the assembly of the first-born who are enrolled in heaven . . . and to the spirits of just men made perfect" (Hebrews 12:22-23 RSV). This sets the church in its proper context. Everytime we meet for worship the whole redeemed church of Christ is here.

Dr. Frank Boreham tells how a few friends of his used to meet together for prayer early on Sunday mornings. At length there came a pouring wet Sunday morning. When one of those sturdy souls came down to eleven o'clock service he was asked, "How many did you have at early prayers this morning?" "Oh, it was grand," was the reply. "We had all the Shining Ones there this morning." He tells also of an old priest trudging home through deep snow after early Mass on the morning of All Saints' Day, being stopped by a man who asked him how many had been at the service. "Millions," he replied. Those two men were conscious of the great cloud of witnesses, the multitude of the redeemed.

I believe in the communion of saints, as a fact and as a force. I believe in the death-defying unity of the family of God. I believe in the fellowship of all the servants of the King in heaven and earth.

> O blest communion, fellowship divine!
> We feebly struggle, they in glory shine;
> Yet all are one in thee, for all are thine.

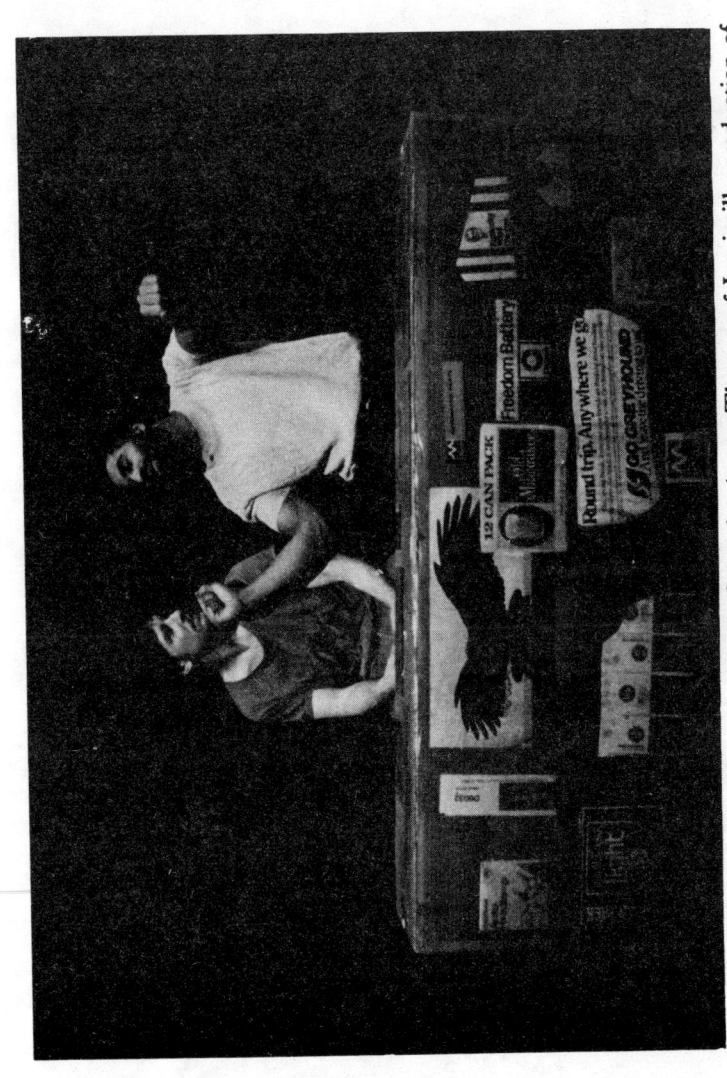

Ben Siegler and Geoffrey Ewing in a scene from the Actors Theatre of Louisville production of "T BONE N WEASEL."

T BONE N WEASEL

A PLAY

By
JON KLEIN

DRAMATISTS
PLAY SERVICE
INC.

© Copyright, 1987, by Jon Klein

CAUTION: Professionals and amateurs are hereby warned that T BONE N WEASEL is subject to a royalty. It is fully protected under the copyright laws of the United States of America, and of all countries covered by the International Copyright Union (including the Dominion of Canada and the rest of the British Commonwealth), and of all countries covered by the Pan-American Copyright Convention and the Universal Copyright Convention, and of all countries with which the United States has reciprocal copyright relations. All rights, including professional, amateur, motion picture, recitation, lecturing, public reading, radio broadcasting, television, video or sound taping, all other forms of mechanical or electronic reproduction, such as information storage and retrieval systems and photocopying, and the rights of translation into foreign languages, are strictly reserved. Particular emphasis is laid upon the question of readings, permission for which must be secured from the author's agent in writing.

The stage performance rights in T BONE N WEASEL (other than first class rights) are controlled exclusively by the DRAMATISTS PLAY SERVICE, INC., 440 Park Avenue South, New York, N.Y. 10016. No professional or non-professional performance of the play (excluding first class professional performance) may be given without obtaining in advance the written permission of the DRAMATISTS PLAY SERVICE, INC., and paying the requisite fee.

Inquiries concerning all other rights should be addressed to Lois Berman, 240 West 44th Street, New York, N.Y. 10036.

SPECIAL NOTE

All groups receiving permission to produce T BONE N WEASEL are required (1) to give credit to the author as sole and exclusive author of the play in all programs distributed in connection with performances of the play and in all instances in which the title of the play appears for purposes of advertising, publicizing or otherwise exploiting the play and/or a production thereof; the name of the author must appear on a separate line, in which no other name appears, immediately beneath the title and in size of type equal to the largest letter used for the title of the play, and (2) to give the following acknowledgment in all programs distributed in connection with performances of the play:

"Professional premiere at Actors Theatre of Louisville"
and
"Originally produced by Quicksilver Stage, Minneapolis, MN"
and
"T BONE N WEASEL was chosen for circulation by Plays in Process, a project of Theatre Communications Group, Inc., the national organization for the nonprofit professional theatre."

The poem "Fat Scrubble" is from GROWING UP SOUTHERN, edited by Chris Mayfield. Copyright © 1981 by Institute for Southern Studies. Reprinted by permission of Pantheon Books, a Division of Random House, Inc.

For Dietz

T BONE N WEASEL was originally developed and given a staged reading at Midwest Playlabs in August, 1986.

T BONE N WEASEL was first produced by Quicksilver Stage of Minneapolis from December 11, 1986 through January 4, 1987. It was directed by Steven Dietz; the design was by Lori Sullivan. The cast was as follows:

T-BONE................................. James Williams
WEASEL .... Tim Danz
MR. FERGUS, HAPPY SAM, REVEREND GLUCK,
LEMUEL CLAYBORNE, VERNA MAE BEAUFORT,
OFFICER KLAMP, DOC TATUM, BROTHER TIM,
RAINCOAT............................... Julian Bailey

T BONE N WEASEL received its professional premiere at the Actors Theatre of Louisville in the Humana Festival of New American Plays, February 18 through March 28, 1987. It was directed by Steven Dietz; the set design was by Paul Owen; the costume design was by Frances Kenny; the lighting design was by Jeff Hill; and the sound design was by David A. Strang. The cast was as follows:

T-BONE .... Geoffrey Ewing
WEASEL .... Ben Siegler
MR. FERGUS, HAPPY SAM, REVEREND GLUCK,
LEMUEL CLAYBORNE, VERNA MAE BEAUFORT,
OFFICER KLAMP, DOC TATUM, BROTHER TIM,
RAINCOAT .... William McNulty

CHARACTERS
(Three men)

T-BONE — Black man, mid thirties.

WEASEL — White man, younger than T-Bone.

MR. FERGUS
HAPPY SAM
REVEREND GLUCK
LEMUEL CLAYBORNE
VERNA MAE BEAUFORT..... all characters played by the same actor.
OFFICER KLAMP
DOC TATUM
BROTHER TIM
RAINCOAT

TIME

The present.

PLACE

The backroads of South Carolina.

AUTHOR'S NOTE

The reader will notice that this script contains no stage directions. This is not intended to mystify directors and producers. I wrote this play in such a way as to free directors and designers to use their own staging concepts rather than mine. Indeed, I have no set idea of how to stage this play. I've seen two directors handle the script very differently, and both approaches seemed entirely valid. However, my experience with productions of the play enables me to supply a few general hints which I hope will be helpful.

In writing T BONE N WEASEL, I wanted it to be a play that relied almost exclusively on the actors. This play should not be about the technical magic of the theatre. It should be about *performing* — both on stage and in the rather hostile environment of the play.

The location titles (including "Intermission") are a crucial part of the play and must be incorporated in the production. At Actors Theatre of Louisville, they were announced as voice-overs as the lights came up on each scene. At Studio Arena Theatre in Buffalo, a visual device was used that suggested the destination scroll on a bus. Being able to read the titles seemed to make a difference to the audience, who responded to them more frequently in the Studio Arena production.

The titles do not describe the scenes. They simply indicate, as briefly as possible, the location of each scene. Since the audience are constantly being told where they are, there is no need to show the locale in any realistic way. In addition, there just isn't the time to "set" each scene. Therefore, the best design is probably a general unit set that allows for speed and ease. The same applies to costume changes. Whether the third actor (who plays multiple roles) has a total costume change for each character, or is using a single prop or costume piece to indicate the change, he must transform as quickly and smoothly as possible.

AUTHOR'S NOTE
(continued)

This play uses several cinematic techniques, similar to those found in Shakespeare's HENRY V. The scenes must flow as seamlessly as a well-edited film sequence. Therefore, using blackouts to separate each scene from the next may not be the best solution.

He swallows buildings, the universe, the whole planet
His mouth burns up when he drinks the sun like a Coke
He has three heads so he can see everywhere he goes
He has rubberband legs and one plastic leg
He's so round he can hardly hold himself to the ground
Gravity and ropes freeze him there
He's a good monster, for when someone robs the bank
before the thief can get caught he swallows the robber,
   the building and the money.

>   —Class poem, Grade 1, Mossy Oaks Elementary

T BONE N WEASEL

A STOLEN BUICK ON U.S. 21

WEASEL. It aint me... it aint me... I aint no fohtunate son... naw naw naw...
T-BONE. Dont sing along man.
WEASEL. *(Long pause.)* Sa good song.
T-BONE. Yeah but you suck.
WEASEL. *(Pause.)* I know that.
T-BONE. *(Pause.)* Which way. We got four directions.
WEASEL. Head south. *(Pause.)* The hell you doin.
T-BONE. Huh.
WEASEL. Watch it.
T-BONE. You tryin to say.
WEASEL. The way you drivin.
T-BONE. Whats wrong with it?
WEASEL. Jest that I be feelin a tad too familiar with the good folk in the neighborin lane. Close enough to shake hands an trade spit.
T-BONE. Aint use to power steerin.
WEASEL. How many times I gotta tell you. Only steal cars you know how to *drive*. But no, you keep goin after this uppity Buick shit. We shoulda grabbed that Chevette.
T-BONE. Pore mans car.
WEASEL. I know what you own, T-Bone. I saw you put it all in this here glove compartment.
T-BONE. Jest rest yer features. I got my pride.
WEASEL. Pride? Lessee. Map o South Caroline. Somebodys comb. Box o Trojans—what you keep these for, luck? Bout twenny-seven dollas and half a Moon Pie. Nope. Dont see no pride.
T-BONE. I said lay off.

WEASEL. Now where would a man like you hide his pride? I got it. In the gas tank.
T-BONE. I mean it Weasel you lay off or Im gonna cloud up and rain all over you.
WEASEL. I hear a lotta thunder but I dont feel a drop.
T-BONE. That chews it. You the expert you drive.
WEASEL. Whacha doin T-Bone get yer hands back on this wheel.
T-BONE. You doin fine without me. We gonna change seats.
WEASEL. I aint never drove before look at my hands shake.
T-BONE. Look to me like Im in the presence of a genuine ace long distance road runner.
WEASEL. I dont know how.
T-BONE. Thass right you dont know how jest like you dont know how to read or write or clean your teeth once a year or put a piece o soap to yer face or spell yer own goddamn *name* fer Chrissake.
WEASEL. Come own T-Bone take this wheel back we gonna end up somebodys hood ownament.
T-BONE. Say pleez.
WEASEL. Pleez you slapassed slack-twisted strut fart.
T-BONE. Awright jest member. Pays to be nice.
WEASEL. *(Pause.)* Need a drink. My throat thinks my heads cut off.
T-BONE. Likker stoer near Blythewood. Saw the sign. "De Sto." Bout as funny as a three legged dog.
WEASEL. Hyeh hyeh hyeh hyeh.
T-BONE. I mean it aint funny.
WEASEL. Oh. *(Pause.)* Whats the name o this sto?
T-BONE. De Sto.
WEASEL. Right whats it called.
T-BONE. Thass it. D, e, s, t, o. Hillbilly way o sayin the stoer. Downright condensational.
WEASEL. What is.
T-BONE. De Sto.
WEASEL. What bout it.
T-BONE. Hell you cant spell why I waste my time jawin I

10

dont know.
WEASEL. Me neither.
T-BONE. Its an insult, thass what. Sayin folk go roun talkin like ignorant crackers.
WEASEL. Im hungry.
T-BONE. Godforsaken South Carolina sandlappers. Puttin up signs like that its a goddamn insult to educative people.
WEASEL. What is.
T-BONE. The sign.
WEASEL. What sign.
T-BONE. De Sto.
WEASEL. What bout it.
T-BONE. Thass another thing Weasel seem like all I do with you is *explain* shit.
WEASEL. All I know is I aint the one goin into conniptions over some damn road sign. You ever read a book they gonna have to tie you down.
T-BONE. You pass right by that likker stoer if it wasnt fer me.
WEASEL. Hell I would.
T-BONE. How you gonna know yer there?
WEASEL. Got a system.
T-BONE. System.
WEASEL. Thass right. Little windows mean beer by the can. Big windows mean beer by the bottle. No windows an flashin lights mean beer on tap. But you might have to kill somebody to git it.
T-BONE. You learn to read you wont have to guess these things.
WEASEL. Aint guessin. Ive developed my observational powers. That, fer example, is a little girl. On her way to school Id say. On account o the books shes carryin.
T-BONE. Hell of a talent.
WEASEL. Jest takes a little concentratin. Now that theres a barn, an thats somebodys wash hangin out to dry, and up head a ways some kinda big tree, an thats a raven. Or else a crow.
T-BONE. Whats this?

WEASEL. Thass yer fist in my face.
T-BONE. You sure? You concentratin?
WEASEL. Aint causin no harm, T-Bone. Jest passin time.
T-BONE. Jest dont pass it my way. *(Pause.)* This is it. De Sto.
WEASEL. What I tell you. Big windows.
T-BONE. No cars. Looks closed.
WEASEL. Saw somebody in there.
T-BONE. Think yer right.
WEASEL. Hey where you goin.
T-BONE. We comin back.
WEASEL. Im thirsty.
T-BONE. Said we be back. Dig out that black-eyed susan o yours.
WEASEL. Say what?
T-BONE. Your piece.
WEASEL. What you want?
T-BONE. Pull out your rod. Lets have a look.
WEASEL. You wanna see my dick?
T-BONE. The *gun*, dammit. Gimme the gun.
WEASEL. Well why dont you *say* so. Gimme this pull out yer *rod* shit.
T-BONE. Jest hand it here.
WEASEL. Minute there thought I was back in the penitentiary.
T-BONE. This thing loaded?
WEASEL. Hell I dunno.
T-BONE. Whens the last time you used it?
WEASEL. Aint never used it.
T-BONE. Never *used* it?
WEASEL. Im least as handy with that .32 as you are with this Buick.
T-BONE. You ever shoot anybody?
WEASEL. I dont keep track o them things. *(Pause.)* Owww leggo leggo leggo.
T-BONE. Look here Weasel. You said you was my man.

WEASEL. I am I am leggo leggo.
T-BONE. I aint so sure bout you.
WEASEL. I gave you references.
T-BONE. They all servin time.
WEASEL. Aint my fault shit that hurts T-Bone.
T-BONE. Dont tell me. Dont tell me I aint spent two weeks lookin fer talent jest to end up with some kinda bum with a head fulla stump water.
WEASEL. I aint gonna tell you that ow.
T-BONE. Dont tell me my partner has feathers on his legs.
WEASEL. Im with you T-Bone.
T-BONE. Thass good Weasel. Otherwise I might be obliged to rearrange yer face.
WEASEL. No need fer that been done three time awready oww shit.
T-BONE. You tell me how I kin trust you I let you go.
WEASEL. I *been* shot does that help?
T-BONE. Where?
WEASEL. Greenville.
T-BONE. I mean where on you.
WEASEL. Left ear.
T-BONE. *(Pause.)* Holy shit took a piece out dint they.
WEASEL. Got me runnin. *(Pause.)* Thanks T-Bone.
T-BONE. Sokay.
WEASEL. Hell of a grip there.
T-BONE. Who shot you. The law?
WEASEL. My dad.
T-BONE. Wha for?
WEASEL. Tryin to member. Think I set fire to his car.
T-BONE. Goddamn.
WEASEL. It was a Buick.
T-BONE. I countin on you Weasel. We gonna go back an take De Sto.
WEASEL. It aint even lunchtime yet.
T-BONE. It jest waitin for us. Daylight dont matter to me.
WEASEL. That how you got sent to Black River?

13

T-BONE. How many times *you* been in prison?
WEASEL. Dunno. I try to arrange it roun the holidays.
T-BONE. What they get you for?
WEASEL. Lessee. Think the last time was attempted robbery.
T-BONE. Armed?
WEASEL. Hell no. Aint *that* fond o the pen. Like to keep my visits short.
T-BONE. Had to scare em somehow.
WEASEL. Sure did. They emptied all the cash drawers.
T-BONE. How you manage that?
WEASEL. Threatened to take off all my clothes. Hell they threw money at me.
T-BONE. Shit. I wanted skilled labor.
WEASEL. Im more of an idea man.
T-BONE. This dont go right you gonna be more of a dead man. Now heres the plan. I pack the heat.
WEASEL. Heat?
T-BONE. The gun. Now you go in to buy somethin an I keep the feller at the register entertained.
WEASEL. What do I buy?
T-BONE. I dont care. Jest dont act like a bum. Show some class.
WEASEL. Night Train.
T-BONE. Fine. Now bring it up to the register. Soons he opens the drawer, I flash my iron.
WEASEL. What iron.
T-BONE. The *gun*, dammit.
WEASEL. You got somethin gainst the word?
T-BONE. You dont call a gun a gun.
WEASEL. You dont.
T-BONE. It aint cool. Iffen I been reduced to a life o crime at least I gonna show some style.
WEASEL. Mebbe I should change my clothes.
T-BONE. We grab the cash an go. We keep the car runnin.
WEASEL. How you gonna keep this guy occupied.

T-BONE. I talk to him.
WEASEL. Bout what.
T-BONE. I dunno. Anythin. The weather.
WEASEL. Lemme hear you.
T-BONE. "Hot, aint it?" Hows that.
WEASEL. Jest fine. You gonna last alla three seconds fore you got ants crawlin up yer nose.
T-BONE. You got a suggestion.
WEASEL. Lemme do the talkin.
T-BONE. Ferget it.
WEASEL. You missin a golden oppotunity. Conversatin is my specialty.
T-BONE. Dont I know it. I wanna git outa there fore Saturday. *(Pause.)* There she is. Still empty.
WEASEL. Hope they got Pearl Beer.
T-BONE. Grab that money. Lets go.
WEASEL. Hold on T-Bone.
T-BONE. Come on. Git out.
WEASEL. I been thinkin.
T-BONE. What.
WEASEL. I aint sure but this jest might be a parole violation.
T-BONE. *Out.*

INSIDE DE STO

MR. FERGUS. Come on in boys. Slow day so Im cleanin my rifle.
WEASEL. Lets go.
T-BONE. We be right back.

BACK IN THE BUICK

WEASEL. Id say this calls for a change of plans.
T-BONE. No it dont.
WEASEL. You crazy?
T-BONE. We can still do it. We got a .32.
WEASEL. Thass right. We can blow our own brains out an save him the trouble.
T-BONE. Look he said he was cleanin that thing. Means its empty. Least fer a while.
WEASEL. What you talkin bout. The mans got a firearm in his hands an you gonna stick him up.
T-BONE. Gotta hurry fore he loads it.
WEASEL. One thing, T-Bone. It ever dawn on you if the man aint had no business he probly got no cash in that drawer.
T-BONE. He gotta make change dont he. Gotta be least a hunnerd in there.
WEASEL. That worth you gettin shot?
T-BONE. I get shot you keep the car.
WEASEL. What if *I* get shot.
T-BONE. Awright Weasel. Guess you right. But jest lemme ask you this. What else you gonna do with yer life?
WEASEL. I tell you what I gonna do with my life. I gonna keep it alive fer one thing. I gonna give up this shit, spendin a week drivin roun South Caroline with one eye on the rear view an the other on easy marks, keepin outa sight o the highway patrol an sleepin in the back seat of a car you cant even operate. Met a man at Black River say he be happy to hep me out, mebbe washin dishes, somethin like that. I kin look him up see if he members me, get a job how bout that T-Bone, a bonerfide *job*, somethin you never even stopped to *consider* am I right. A steady paycheck an a roof over my head an reglar hours an holdin my head up as a law-abidin citizen. *(Pause.)*
T-BONE. You ready?
WEASEL. Keep the car runnin. Lets take this sucker.

BACK IN DE STO

T-BONE. Fergot our money.
WEASEL. Keeps it in the glove compartment. Twenny-seven dollas.
MR. FERGUS. Dont wanna lose that.
WEASEL. No sir.
T-BONE. Why dont you jest go pick somethin out.
WEASEL. Will do.
T-BONE. Hot, aint it.
MR. FERGUS. Whats that.
T-BONE. Hot. Hot day.
MR. FERGUS. Wouldnt know. Got an air conditioner.
T-BONE. *(Pause.)* Nice in here.
MR. FERGUS. That sight look straight to you?
WEASEL. Dont shoot! I dont even know him! Picked me up hitchin to Columbia!
T-BONE. He jest fixin the *sight*.
WEASEL. *(Pause.)* I know that.
T-BONE. Dont let him bother you. Guns make him a little rabbitty.
MR. FERGUS. No need for that. Theys a sayin, hows it go. Guns dont kill people. People kill guns. No that aint right. Well, guns, people, it all works out somehow.
T-BONE. You decide what you want?
WEASEL. Not yet. It all looks so *good*.
T-BONE. Put it in gear.
MR. FERGUS. Mebbe I can hep find what you lookin fer.
T-BONE. You stay right there. I see what we want from here. Right in front o his nose.
WEASEL. This thing?
T-BONE. Thass right. Bring it up here.
WEASEL. You say so.
MR. FERGUS. Whats the verdict. Why I declare I aint never sole one o these items. Imported pear brandy.

T-BONE. What the hell is that?
WEASEL. Thass what was in front o me.
MR. FERGUS. Straight from the still. No need to age it. You boys plannin a celebration?
T-BONE. Could say that. How much is it?
MR. FERGUS. Less see. Includin tax, that come to twenny fo dollas an ninedy five cents.
T-BONE. *How* much?
MR. FERGUS. Come from Switzer-land.
WEASEL. Look T-Bone why dont I jest put the damn thing back.
T-BONE. Pay the man. We gonna be makin a withdrawal anyway.
WEASEL. How we gonna do that we aint even got a bank acc-owww leggo leggo.
T-BONE. Pay him.
MR. FERGUS. *(Pause.)* Outa twenny five. *(Pause.)* Doggone cash drawer. Been stickin for days. *(Pause.)* Nope. Cant budge it. See if one o you can open it.
T-BONE. Glad to. *(Pause.)* Son of a *bitch*.
MR. FERGUS. Shoulda had the man out yesterday. What I get fer puttin it off.
T-BONE. Mebbe if I had a rock.
WEASEL. He only owes us a nickel.
T-BONE. Shut up and find a rock Weasel.
MR. FERGUS. Weasel? Used to know a boy back in Greenville called himself Weasel.
WEASEL. Im from Greenville.
T-BONE. No you aint! He aint from Greenville!
WEASEL. Shore I am. Brought up on Palmetto Drive.
MR. FERGUS. William Weasler! Thought I recognized you!
T-BONE. You *know* him?
MR. FERGUS. Shonuff. Use to live cross the street from the Weasler family.
WEASEL. Not Mister Fergus.
MR. FERGUS. The same.

WEASEL. With them Porky Pig imitations.
MR. FERGUS. Uhh th-th-th-that-thats ri-ri-ri-ri-you bet.
WEASEL. I be dogged.
MR. FERGUS. Hows yer dad.
WEASEL. Dead.
MR. FERGUS. Lets see that ear. *(Pause.)* Took a chunk out dint he.
WEASEL. Yes sir.
MR. FERGUS. Still. Shouldna burned his Buick.
WEASEL. I know it.
T-BONE. We got *bizness* here Weasel.
MR. FERGUS. Oh you kin spare a minute with an ole neighbor from Greenville. Hows yer mama.
WEASEL. She killed my dad. I think shes in Utah.
MR. FERGUS. You hear from her say hi from Mr. Fergus.
T-BONE. Hate to break up the social hour.
WEASEL. T-Bone.
T-BONE. Now if you wont mind movin way from the register.
MR. FERGUS. You gonna shoot it open?
T-BONE. Thass the idea.
MR. FERGUS. Preciate the thought boy. But Id rather jest call the serviceman.
T-BONE. You aint got the picture yet, do you.
WEASEL. T-Bone.
T-BONE. This aint for yer *benefit.*
WEASEL. T-Bone.
T-BONE. What the hell *you* want.
WEASEL. Take a listen.
T-BONE. What you talkin bout? I dont hear nuthin.
WEASEL. What I mean. The car aint runnin. The motor gave out. *(Long pause.)* Wanna sip?

THE PARKING LOT

MR. FERGUS. Jest as I figgered.
T-BONE. What is it?
MR. FERGUS. Fan belt broke. New one cost you three fifty.
T-BONE. We aint got three fifty. Spent it all on that damn brandy.
MR. FERGUS. Then you cant afford to tow it. Thats a tough one. Nearest gas stations fifteen miles.
T-BONE. How bout a refund on the pear brandy.
MR. FERGUS. Not with that Greenville boy over there suckin on the bottle.
T-BONE. Damn it Weasel. Now we stuck with a dead car an less than two bucks cash.
WEASEL. This stuff...is worth it.
T-BONE. Now to top that off you drunk.
MR. FERGUS. Theys a car lot down the road a mile. Happy Sams. Mebbe he give you a belt.
WEASEL. No thanks...got plenty.
T-BONE. Get up Weasel you gonna push this car.
WEASEL. You gonna blow it out yer ass.
MR. FERGUS. Mebbe you oughta let him steer.
WEASEL. Thass right. I been practicin.
T-BONE. Get in the car.
MR. FERGUS. Almost forgot. Here you go.
T-BONE. Whats this.
MR. FERGUS. Your change. Had a nickel in my pocket. Looks like your lucky da-da-de-de-de-da-de-day.

HAPPY SAM'S USED CARS

T-BONE. You can let go the wheel now.
WEASEL. Hot damn. Got this steerin *down*.
T-BONE. Here he comes. I do the talkin.
WEASEL. Fine by me. Gotta use the facility. Time to recycle my shorts.
HAPPY SAM. *(Long pause.)* Give you a hunnerd.
T-BONE. What.
HAPPY SAM. Fer the Buick.
T-BONE. Aint fer sale.
HAPPY SAM. Then fuck off.
T-BONE. Hold on. Wheres Happy Sam.
HAPPY SAM. You got him.
T-BONE. Happy Sam?
HAPPY SAM. Got a problem with that? Oh I know what yer thinkin, you jest dont seem all that happy, Sam. Well it hard to be happy all the goddamn time. You try spendin day after day dealin with the dregs o humanity, people so low they could wear a top hat and still walk under the belly of a snake. Like people who push busted Buicks on my lot.
T-BONE. I jest need a fan belt.
HAPPY SAM. Course you do every goddamn car comes on this lot needs a fan belt an Im the one has to put em on.
T-BONE. You got one I can use?
HAPPY SAM. This look like a *garage* boy you can look around as far as the eye can see an you wont find no mechanic. Its jest me, two pimple-face boys couldnt sell a fly to a spider, an a doberman I keep on hand to chew the ass off people like you. Aint got no fan belts anyway.
T-BONE. Could you look?
HAPPY SAM. I know what I got here its *my* goddamn lot. I got cars an calendars. An you dont get a calendar less you buy a car.
T-BONE. Look its an emergency.

HAPPY SAM. Lifes an emergency. You fucked up.
T-BONE. Awright what if I did. Can I jest borrow a fan belt off one o these ol cars?
HAPPY SAM. Thass the problem with this country too many handouts. Its a national disgrace an I aint gonna be no contributin factor.
T-BONE. Listen. We need some cash.
HAPPY SAM. Well dont that make you the wonder attraction o Richland County. People be linin up for miles jest to take a look at you.
T-BONE. Okay. The Buick.
HAPPY SAM. A hunnerd.
T-BONE. You know what I paid for this car?
HAPPY SAM. Probly a hunnerd less than my offer.
T-BONE. You sinuatin Im a car thief?
HAPPY SAM. Got the registration? *(Pause.)* One hunnerd.
T-BONE. Please mister.
HAPPY SAM. Happy.
T-BONE. Happy. Check it out. Its gotta be worth a few grand at the least. Its prackly new.
HAPPY SAM. Its broke. Saw you push it on the lot.
T-BONE. Thass the fan belt!
HAPPY SAM. So get it fixed. Then I look at it.
T-BONE. I aint got the *cash*.
HAPPY SAM. Look you tryin to sell me a car that dont even *run*. You lucky I dont sic the doberman. *(Long pause.)*
T-BONE. Two thousand.
HAPPY SAM. One hunnerd.
T-BONE. One thousand.
HAPPY SAM. One hunnerd.
T-BONE. Five hunnerd.
HAPPY SAM. One hunnerd.
T-BONE. Four hunnerd.
HAPPY SAM. One hunnerd.
T-BONE. *(Pause.)* Three hunnerd.
HAPPY SAM. One hunnerd.

T-BONE. Two hunnerd.
HAPPY SAM. One hunnerd.
T-BONE. Hunnerd fifty.
HAPPY SAM. One hunnerd.
T-BONE. *(Pause.)* Hunnerd twenny five.
HAPPY SAM. One hunnerd.
T-BONE. Hunnerd twenny.
HAPPY SAM. One hunnerd.
T-BONE. Hunnerd ten.
HAPPY SAM. One hunnerd.
T-BONE. *(Pause.)* One hunnerd *five*.
HAPPY SAM. *(Pause.)* Awright Im a reasonable man. Here you go. Twenny, forety, sixty, eighty, one hunnerd an five dollas.
T-BONE. Dont I sign anythin?
HAPPY SAM. Shore if you want. Course that sends yer name to the state courthouse along with the record o transfer.
T-BONE. Never mind. Jest lemme ask you somethin.
HAPPY SAM. Fire away.
T-BONE. How much you gonna sell this car for?
HAPPY SAM. Oh Id say bout five thousand.
T-BONE. WHAT?
HAPPY SAM. Course I gotta fix that fan belt first. Thanks boy. You jest made Sam very happy.

KILLIAN CITY LIMITS

T-BONE. Killian city limits.
WEASEL. You jest said that.
T-BONE. I did?
WEASEL. Hope theys a donut shop in town. My stomachs wamblin an my feet are draggly.
T-BONE. All that fool pear brandy.
WEASEL. Thass right, go head an critisize. Hope you notice how Im sidlin way from the fack that you done give way our only means o transport. Hope you preciate how I dont bring that up.
T-BONE. You bringin it up now aint you.
WEASEL. But I aint makin no judgment. I could be tellin you how that was dumber than takin a piss on a lectric fence.
T-BONE. Awright awright lemme have some o that Swiss pear juice.
WEASEL. Dont see why not you paid fer it.
T-BONE. *(Pause.)* Boy that fix yer plumbin dont it.
WEASEL. Where is Switzer-land anyhow.
T-BONE. Some place in Yurp. They got lots o mountains an cheese an chocklit and clocks an shit. I seen pictures.
WEASEL. They got women?
T-BONE. You know that gal on those cans o powder coco? With the blonde hair an the puffed up shirt?
WEASEL. Right look like she be herdin goats or somethin.
T-BONE. Thass what they look like.
WEASEL. Shit. I gonna move there.
T-BONE. Lets do it Weasel.
WEASEL. Do what.
T-BONE. Go to Switzer-land.
WEASEL. You mean it?
T-BONE. You an me. Leave South Carolina to the sandlappers.
WEASEL. Now you talkin.
T-BONE. Put er there.

WEASEL. *(Long pause.)* Aint got a chance do we.
T-BONE. Hell no.
WEASEL. Shit.
T-BONE. We outa pear juice.
WEASEL. Things come crashin down *fast* dont they.
T-BONE. Lets get some beer.
WEASEL. An donuts.
T-BONE. I wanna real meal. We go to the store and get us some Spam.
WEASEL. I just now figgered it out. Its yer name.
T-BONE. What bout it.
WEASEL. Why Im hungry all the damn time. I keep thinkin bout steak. That really yer name?
T-BONE. Naw.
WEASEL. What is it.
T-BONE. Pends on the state.
WEASEL. State o what.
T-BONE. State o the country. In Geohgia Im Leland Johnson. In Loosiana Im Hakim Lefevre.
WEASEL. But whats yer *real* name.
T-BONE. Oh that. Dont rightly member. Use so many. I pretty much ruled out Bob. Aint many black folk name they kids Bob.
WEASEL. Where you git T-Bone.
T-BONE. Take a gander at my shin.
WEASEL. *(Pause.)* Nasty lookin scar.
T-BONE. Folks owned a nearsighted rat terrier. Was playin on a swing set an he thought someone was throwin him a steak bone.
WEASEL. He chew yer leg?
T-BONE. Wouldnt let go. My daddy had to borry a bitch in heat from down the street jest to distract him.
WEASEL. He shoot the dog?
T-BONE. Naw. Jest fed him reglar.
WEASEL. Damn thing look like my ear.
T-BONE. Life aint easy.

WEASEL. Dont seem right.
T-BONE. Aint right.
WEASEL. Well it gotta stop sometime T-Bone. I mean ever since my mama grab that .32 and blew off the back o my dads head while he was eatin breakfast. Things jest dont seem to let up. Whacha stop fer.
T-BONE. She use this gun.
WEASEL. Yep. Talk bout a mess. Good thing the table was formica.
T-BONE. Dont tell me. Dont tell me I been carryin roun a *murder* weapon.
WEASEL. Well if you wanna put it that way oww leggo leggo.
T-BONE. I almost *use* this thing back in Blythewood. I thought it was clean.
WEASEL. *Is* clean. Only been used once. Oww will you leggo.
T-BONE. How you git this thing.
WEASEL. Come UPS right after I got outa Black River.
T-BONE. She *mail* it to you?
WEASEL. Thass right now leggo o me.
T-BONE. We gotta git rid of it.
WEASEL. Wish you quit grabbin me like that. Give it here. *(Pause.)* There. Now you happy?
T-BONE. Dont tell me. Dont tell me you jest threw it off a bridge with our fingerprints all over the damn thing. Dont tell me you threw that gun.
WEASEL. Okay. I dint throw no gun. I threw a *rod*.

A RAVINE UNDER COUNTY 555

T-BONE. You find it?
WEASEL. Not yet. Amazin all the artyfacks you find under a bypass. Look at this. A toilet seat.
T-BONE. Jest look fer that .32.
WEASEL. Heres a damn washin machine. An a dryer next to it. Could open a laudermat under this bridge.
T-BONE. We be needin one after we wade through this shit.
WEASEL. Hold on.
T-BONE. See it?
WEASEL. Some kinda tellygram.
T-BONE. Bring it here. *(Pause.)* "You could already be a winner." Some kinda sweepstakes.
WEASEL. An somebody threw it *away?*
T-BONE. Junk.
WEASEL. Hey give it here.
T-BONE. Theys millions o those things. Only meant to get pore folks hopes up. See that word? That say "occu-pant." Mean they dont even care *who* gets it.
WEASEL. Then they dont mind I keep it. Might come in handy.
T-BONE. Suit yourself. *(Pause.)* Somebody done settled down here. Campfire, wood shelter. Mus be a tramp nearby.
REVEREND GLUCK. Aint no tramp. Aint no vagrant, transint or ragpicker neither.
WEASEL. Thats my gun.
REVEREND GLUCK. Get yer hands up.
T-BONE. Mean no harm mister.
WEASEL. Jesus Mary an Joseph.
REVEREND GLUCK. Dont talk to me bout Jesus. I read the Bible ever day an I know what it take to save souls.
T-BONE. Course you do mister.
REVEREND GLUCK. Reverend. Reverend Gluck. Doctor o Sacred Theology an Minister o the Holy Church o the Ravine. The

Lawd Awmighty bless you an preserve you now an forever.
WEASEL & T-BONE. Amen.
REVEREND GLUCK. Now empty yer pockets.
WEASEL. But thass my gun. I threw if off the bridge.
REVEREND GLUCK. Then it aint yers no more. Anythin tossed off this bridge comes a sacrifisial offerin to the Lawd an church property. As Gods personally ordained minister its my duty to gather up these holy gifts. An to accept donations in His name.
T-BONE. Aint got nothin to give.
REVEREND GLUCK. That true Lawd? *(Pause.)* Sorry. The Lawd say you holdin out on Him. He say fer me to look in yer shoes.
T-BONE. Its all we got.
REVEREND GLUCK. Have to give up earthly possessions if you gonna enter the gates o Heaven. Now take em off. *(Pause.)* Theys a lotta hate in the world, my sons. Lotta injustice. Cruelty. Dishonesty. Sometimes it hard fer me to git up in the moanin an face another day. But jest when my spirits sink to the point where I begin to turn my back on the Lawd, there outa the sky come flyin a spiritual offerin. Some days its a dead cat. Some days its a rusted engine. Some days its some kind o poison chemical. But all things are precious in the eyes o the Lawd, and they give me the strength to go on. An that goes fer your - how much you got there?
T-BONE. A hunnerd an five dollas.
REVEREND GLUCK. The Lawd is pleased. Put it in the collection plate. Now you.
WEASEL. All I got is a card fer social security.
REVEREND GLUCK. Aint no such thing. Put it in the plate. Whats that in yer hand.
WEASEL. Sweepstakes offer.
REVEREND GLUCK. Keep it. Awready got one somewheres. Now lessee...William Weasler. And...dint ketch yer name.
T-BONE. Dint give it to you.
REVEREND GLUCK. Aint necessary. The Lawd members his chosen ones. Now off with you. *(Pause.)* Run. *(Pause.)* Thass it.

Spread the word. Service on Sunday! Nine o clock sharp! Come early! The car seats fill up fast!

THE BASEMENT OF ST. BONIFACE

T-BONE. Cant sleep there.
WEASEL. Dont worry bout it.
T-BONE. All the beds taken. Gotta use the floor.
WEASEL. Had a chat with the head nun. Said I could use this one till the guy gits back from the blood bank.
T-BONE. What then.
WEASEL. I worked it out.
T-BONE. Dont say I dint warn you.
WEASEL. Not a bad meal. Coulda done without the Kool Aid.
T-BONE. Its humiliatin. Never spent a night in a shelter an I hope I never do again.
WEASEL. Got a lead on a job. Woman in Lugoff need help.
T-BONE. We go there tomorrow.
WEASEL. Time fer a change in luck. That preacher was past strange.
T-BONE. Shoulda taken Happy Sam. Would have without the doberman.
WEASEL. Countrys gone to shit ever since Creedence Clearwater broke up.
T-BONE. You an that damn band. Theys other bands jest as good.
WEASEL. Name one.
T-BONE. I dunno...the Beatles.
WEASEL. T-Bone. Look at me. *(Pause.)* Tell me you dont mean that. *(Pause.)*
T-BONE. Awright I hate the Beatles.
CLAYBORNE. Hey. You. Thass. Mmmmy. Bed.
T-BONE. Now you in fer it.
WEASEL. Yer name Lemuel Clayborne?
CLAYBORNE. Yeah. Sssso. What.
WEASEL. Been waitin fer you. To deliver this tellygram.
CLAYBORNE. Fer. Mmmme?

WEASEL. From yer sister.
CLAYBORNE. Aint. Got. Nnnno. Sis. Ter.
WEASEL. I mean yer brother.
CLAYBORNE. Nnnna. Than?
WEASEL. Thass right. Nathan. Here you go.
CLAYBORNE. *(Pause.)* Whats. It. Ssssay?
WEASEL. Give it back. I read it to you. *(Pause.)* "Brother Lemuel. Stop."
CLAYBORNE. Sssstop. What.
WEASEL. Thass jest tellygram talk. I leave out the stops. "Brother Lemuel. Come home now. Important."
CLAYBORNE. To. Nnnnight?
WEASEL. "Leave tonight. Nathan."
CLAYBORNE. He. Throwed. Mmmme. Out.
WEASEL. Guess all is forgiven. Better skedaddle.
CLAYBORNE. Thanks. Mmmmis. Ter.
WEASEL. Best o luck. *(Long pause.)* That boy was *slow*.
T-BONE. Thass a terrible thing to do.
WEASEL. Folk belong with their fambly.
T-BONE. He jest git throwed out agin.
WEASEL. Mebbe. Mebbe not.
T-BONE. You slicker than goose shit, you know that?
WEASEL. Night T-Bone.
T-BONE. Night.
WEASEL. *(Long pause.)* T-Bone.
T-BONE. What.
WEASEL. You miss yer home.
T-BONE. No.
WEASEL. You sure.
T-BONE. Shut up an go to sleep.
WEASEL. *(Long pause.)* T-Bone.
T-BONE. What.
WEASEL. What yer name really.
T-BONE. Dunno.
WEASEL. You gotta know.
T-BONE. Dammit Weasel you dont pipe down I come over there

an rip yer arm off.
WEASEL. *(Long pause.)* T-Bone.
T-BONE. *What.*
WEASEL. How bout a goodnight kiss oww leggo leggo.

VERNA MAE BEAUFORT'S FARM

WEASEL. Pardon us maam. This here the Beaufort place?
VERNA MAE. Thass right.
WEASEL. We was hearin as to how you might could use a coupla hired hands.
VERNA MAE. Take off yer shirts.
WEASEL. *(Pause.)* Scuse me maam?
VERNA MAE. Yer shirts. Both o you. *(Pause.)* Awright. Youll do.
WEASEL. Whats the job.
VERNA MAE. Need some bird minders.
WEASEL. Hens what I tell you T-Bone that right up our alley.
VERNA MAE. No hens. Bobolinks. Gotta chase em outa the rice field. Youll git yer feet wet.
WEASEL. That all there is? Chasin rice birds?
T-BONE. Whats the pay.
VERNA MAE. Show some respeck boy. Miss Beaufort.
T-BONE. Sorry. Miss Beaufort.
VERNA MAE. Three dollas an hour. Work sunup to sunset an the rest o the nights yours to do as you plese. Plus johnny cake fer lunch an chicken bog fer supper. an a place to bed down in the barn.
WEASEL. Chicken bog you say. Souns reasonable.
VERNA MAE. Course yer boy eats outside.
T-BONE. I aint his -
WEASEL. We preciate it Miss Beaufort. We shore do need the work.
VERNA MAE. Gotta be here through harvest. I expeck seven mortars a day from each o you.
T-BONE. Now hold on.
WEASEL. That fine by us.
VERNA MAE. Awright then. Can both start out in the paddy till I ring the bell.

WEASEL. That mean lunch time?
VERNA MAE. That mean I want you come see me personal. Got another task. Yer boy can stay with them birds.
T-BONE. Miss Beaufort.
VERNA MAE. Yes?
T-BONE. My name...my name is Tom.
VERNA MAE. *(Pause.)* Dont need yer name boy. Aint ever gonna use it.

8:00 IN THE PADDY

WEASEL. Chicken bog. Hot damn.
T-BONE. Dont care what she feeds us. Aint gonna be no womans slave. She stomp down ugly to boot.
WEASEL. She aint that bad.
T-BONE. I tell you she could turn a train down a dirt road.
WEASEL. Look at them rice birds. Fly you birds! Eeeaayyaaa!
T-BONE. Yaaahooo!
WEASEL. Hoooo birds! Git!
WEASEL. These little fellers some kinda brave. Keep comin back fer more.
T-BONE. Haaaahh!
WEASEL. Grab up some rocks.
T-BONE. Weasel.
WEASEL. Got one in the wing see that.
T-BONE. Weasel. Askin you somethin.
WEASEL. Yeeeehawwwww what.
T-BONE. I wanna know where you stand.
WEASEL. Right here what kinda fool question -
T-BONE. I mean on color. *(Pause.)* Talkin bout this *thing* man. What people *say* bout it.
WEASEL. What you goin on bout T-Bone.
T-BONE. Im askin what it *mean* to you.
WEASEL. Aint never thought bout it.
T-BONE. *Course* you aint man that cause you the white man you dont have to give it no *thought* see what Im sayin.
WEASEL. What the hell is *with* you. We got work to do.
T-BONE. *(Pause.)* Hyyaaaaaaaahh you rice birds!
WEASEL. Jesus T-Bone slow down you got the whole day head o you.
T-BONE. Yaaaaaaaaaaaaaaawwwwwwwwww!
WEASEL. *Stop* it.
T-BONE. *(Pause.)* Theys the bell.

WEASEL. You all right?
T-BONE. Go on see what she wants.
WEASEL. I be back soons I can.
T-BONE. *(Long pause.)* God damn birds.

10:30

WEASEL. T-Bone? T-Bone! Where the hell are you. Damn bobolinks. Hyaaah! What the - T-Bone? Get up yer face outa that mud fore you drown. Come on. Roll over. *(Pause.)* Jesus Mary an Joseph. *(Pause.)*
T-BONE. Yiiiiiii!
WEASEL. Aiiiieee!
T-BONE. Hee hee hee the look on yer face.
WEASEL. Damn it T-Bone.
T-BONE. That set yer hair dint it.
WEASEL. Aint in the mood for yer shenanigans.
T-BONE. Damn Weasel you look like somethin the hogs left behind. What she got you doin anyhow.
WEASEL. Dont wanna talk bout it.
T-BONE. Whatever it is you shore dont look dirty. What kinda job - *(Pause.)* Weasel.
WEASEL. What.
T-BONE. You *servicin* that woman.
WEASEL. Said I don wanna discuss it.
T-BONE. Weasel. That woman could gag a maggot.
WEASEL. I tell you T-Bone you lemme alone or else I gonna - whats that.
T-BONE. *(Pause.)* The bell.
WEASEL. No. God no.
T-BONE. Lets get out here Weasel. Theys hair in the butter.
WEASEL. Cant leave.
T-BONE. Why not.
WEASEL. Chicken bog. *(Pause.)* The bell.
T-BONE. Weasel. If you gotta do this.
WEASEL. My mind is made.
T-BONE. Dont let her get on top. An think bout Switzerland.

11:45

WEASEL. T-Bone.
T-BONE. Over here.
WEASEL. Cant make it over there. My legs are shot. *(Pause.)* No. No. Tell me Im hearin things.
T-BONE. Its the bell.
WEASEL. Kill me now T-Bone. Slit my throat.
T-BONE. Could jest be the johnny cake.
WEASEL. Aint ever gonna eat. Jest gonna shag her till I die. *(Pause.)* T-Bone.
T-BONE. Why you lookin at me like that.
WEASEL. You gotta take my place.
T-BONE. Have you lost yer ever lovin *mind.* You couldn't get me in there with a cattle prod. *(Pause.)* Dont cry Weasel. *(Pause.)* Shit. Whats that woman gonna do when a black man walk into her bedroom.

11:52

T-BONE. Lets go Weasel.
WEASEL. Where you off to?
T-BONE. I got her purse an shes got a shotgun. Come *own*.
WEASEL. Why you always pull this shit at mealtimes.
T-BONE. Run!

A BACK CORNER BOOTH IN THE PONTIAC SNACK HOUSE

WEASEL. Eatin a double cheeseburger be like starin in the face o God.
T-BONE. One could say that.
WEASEL. Wonder they got cheeseburgers in Heaven.
T-BONE. Hard to know.
WEASEL. Aint goin if they dont.
T-BONE. Mama use to say God be havin fish fries on Friday an fried chicken on Sunday.
WEASEL. How bout rest o the time.
T-BONE. Dont eat. No matter since no one ever get hungry.
WEASEL. That hashes it. They gonna have to drag me in screamin.
T-BONE. Aint goin to Heaven so why worry bout it.
WEASEL. Why you so negatory.
T-BONE. Gotta be in a church. We aint mean nuff for the Baptists or rich nuff for the Catlicks.
WEASEL. Theys the Lutherans.
T-BONE. Day they let a black man in be the day God holds Open House.
WEASEL. Might have a better chance if we dint go round robbin folk.
T-BONE. Dont think they heard you in the next county.
WEASEL. I mean it jest dont settle with me takin that purse.
T-BONE. We done *earn* this money Weasel. Dont see you keep from crammin yer jowls with the profits.
WEASEL. Dont mean I *like* it. Say girl. Back here. Hot fudge sundae. With nuts.
T-BONE. You sufferin all right.
WEASEL. It my *conshus* that botherin me T-Bone. All I know is we had a chance at some honest work for a change.
T-BONE. I was her nigger an you was her whore. That what you call honest?

WEASEL. You an me got a different way o lookin at right and wrong. Pass the ketchup.
T-BONE. Hush up. The law comin this way. *(Long pause.)*
OFFICER KLAMP. How do boys. Mind I set a spell. That is if it dont ill convenience you.
WEASEL. Cose not officer. We jest passin through town an came across this pleasant little rest stop.
OFFICER KLAMP. Travellers are you. Roy Klamp. My pleasure. How bout them onion rings house specialty.
WEASEL. Past excellent.
OFFICER KLAMP. Mind if I.
WEASEL. Hep yourself.
OFFICER KLAMP. By chance that wouldnt be your Buick out there.
T-BONE. *(Pause.)* Buick.
WEASEL. We be explorin the fine countryside on foot officer.
OFFICER KLAMP. Jest as well. That back tire mighty low. Well. Better ask roun.
WEASEL. Thanks for the drop in. Take another onion ring with you.
OFFICER KLAMP. Dont mind if I do. By the by, you bein visitors must explain why you boys sittin in the wrong booth.
WEASEL. Wrong booth. Dint realize it be reserved.
OFFICER KLAMP. So you boys wont mind movin to the other section.
WEASEL. Course not officer. What sections that.
OFFICER KLAMP. The colored section. *(Pause.)* Jest kiddin boys haw haw haw haw haw haw haw.
WEASEL. That ones a knee slapper aint it T-Bone. *Aint* it.
T-BONE. Funny.
OFFICER KLAMP. Now thats what I like to see. Good sense o humor.
WEASEL. Nice talkin to you but we better mosey along while the lights good.
OFFICER KLAMP. Now that bring up another little matter. Here I am at the counter enjoyin a mud flop sandwich when I hap-

pen to notice these two boys in the back corner. Course I know ever body in Pontiac so a strange face sorta stands out roun here. An it hits me like a bolt from the blue that these two boys come awful close to matchin a radio scription from the sheriff o Lugoff. Seems Verna Mae Beaufort run into some trouble end up misplacin bout two hunnerd thirty dollas. Now Lawd knows Verna Mae could make a bull freeze in his tracks an his piss turn to ice but still the law *is* the law an you know the rest of it. So now I be faced with a perdickament. One thing I can do is take these boys back to face the wrath of Verna Mae, a sitchyation which make my eyes water jest to think of it. The other choice be to let these boys jest hand over the money they found to Officer Klamp fer safekeepin. That way ever body gets saved from certain unpleasant consequences. Now heres my trouble. I jest caint make up my mind what I should do. Thought you boys might could give me a little *hep*.

T-BONE. *(Pause.)* How much.

OFFICER KLAMP. No need to split it up. Wouldnt want any o them bills gettin lonesome. *(Pause.)* I do declare. An here I figgured Verna Mae was exaggeratin. Well I hope to ketch up with them purse snatchers soon. You boys have youself a good trip. Tell you what Im in a generous mood. Lunch is on me. An heres some money fer a coupla bus tickets outa Richland County. Cause the next time I see you Im gonna find a reason to bust yer ass. *(Pause.)* These boys gotta run Ruthie. I can take that sundae.

ON THE GREYHOUND

WEASEL. I done had all I can take o this T-Bone.
T-BONE. Jest rest yore eyes Weasel. I sense somethin comin.
WEASEL. What you think it is.
T-BONE. Aint sure. But we be due for a break.

INTERMISSION

EDISTO BEACH AT 3 AM

WEASEL. Unh? Wha? Pfffft. Pffffffffftt.
T-BONE. Some folk tryin to sleep.
WEASEL. Pfffft.
T-BONE. Quit makin like a cat.
WEASEL. Sand in my mouth.
T-BONE. What happen when you roll off the blanket.
WEASEL. Ohhhhh. Oohhhhhhhhhhhhhh.
T-BONE. Feelin sick?
WEASEL. Stomach.
T-BONE. Nother thing wrong with you Weasel never can hold yer likker.
WEASEL. Likker is one thing. Rubbin alcohol an grape juice another matter.
T-BONE. It was Sunday. Now what you tryin to do.
WEASEL. Put on my pants.
T-BONE. Thass yer shirt.
WEASEL. *(Pause.)* I know that.
T-BONE. You still drunk Weasel.
WEASEL. Am not.
T-BONE. Are so look at you caint hardly stand soun like a camel when you talk.
WEASEL. I got *poison* in my system T-Bone poison that you concocted an poured down my throat like it was some kinda damn motor oil. Probly used a funnel.
T-BONE. No body forced you.
WEASEL. Coulda given me a little *warnin,* somethin like "Hey Weasel, what say we drink some o this shit gonna make us die an go into mortar riggis." But no jest cause you in this *mood* to pack it in an visit Charleston Bay face down I gotta go along. Ohhhhh.
T-BONE. You tryin to say.
WEASEL. Sayin you on a *slide* T-Bone you tryin to take me with you got another thought comin. I got *plans* you know lotta stuff I could be doin stead o sleepin on beaches, drinkin cheap wine an

panhandlin people from Milwaukee while they be playin volleyball.

T-BONE. Like what.

WEASEL. Like goin to Columbia an findin a *job* T-Bone. A way to live. Vocation counselor at Black River tell me they got a company there called Service Industry always lookin fer people.

T-BONE. Aint no company Weasel. Service industry mean minimum wage work. Means takin a job where you sell other folk things you never gonna have yourself. They turn it to shit an you clean it up.

WEASEL. Aint like that T-Bone.

T-BONE. Wise up Weasel you live in a dream.

WEASEL. Rather live in a dream than not at all. Somethin in my damn pants what the owww shit owww somethins got me. Look at that look at that—T-Bone a crab a damn *crab* in my pants.

T-BONE. Tole you to roll yer pants legs tight.

WEASEL. Dont you sit there actin like a newborn *chile* you put it there you put it in my pants. Probly hopin it would bite my pecker off so you could use it fer soup.

T-BONE. You bout to have a dog fit Weasel. Sit down.

WEASEL. No Im leavin.

T-BONE. No you aint.

WEASEL. Jest watch me.

T-BONE. You caint last an hour out there. You in some kinda breakdown fever.

WEASEL. Get outa my fuck you *face*.

T-BONE. Caint even cuss right.

WEASEL. Dont touch me. I aint afraid to use this.

T-BONE. *(Pause.)* Where you git that Arkansas toothpick.

WEASEL. This is a *knife*. Aint a Texas sewin needle, a Mississippi pig-sticker or a Kentucky back scratcher. Its a knife a knife a knife a knife a knife now what you gonna do bout it.

T-BONE. Not a damn thing.

WEASEL. Thass good.

T-BONE. See you later.

WEASEL. *(Pause.)* You goin back to sleep.

T-BONE. Might as well.
WEASEL. Dark out there aint it.
T-BONE. Usually is this time o night.
WEASEL. Mebbe I should wait til mornin.
T-BONE. Mebbe you should.
WEASEL. Hell T-Bone you really gonna settle fer this?
T-BONE. *(Pause.)* I dont settle fer *nothin* man. *(Pause.)* Went fer a swim yesterday. Water was clean blue. Specks o coral washin through my toes. Winnebago pulls up on shore. Family gits out. Man, woman, two little kids with bony knees an big bright eyes. They all dressed up in swimmin outfits, headin fer the water. An the little ones start bouncin on the sand, lettin the waves carry em back an forth an tryin to ketch the seagulls. All of a sudden the mama calls em in an they climb right back into the trailer. Couldn figger this out. I mean they was havin plenty o fun, why cut it short. Then jest fore the mama climb in with the baskets an shut the door, she stop, turn an look straight at my face.
WEASEL. *(Pause.)* What this got to do with me.
T-BONE. Dont give me that man you was right there on the beach.
WEASEL. I dint notice.
T-BONE. This what I talkin bout Weasel. Things go on all the time, right front o yer nose, an you dont ever *see* nothin. Why is that?
WEASEL. Dunno T-Bone. Hard to say.
T-BONE. *(Pause.)* Guess you right. Time to move on.

A CONSTRUCTION SITE IN FROGMORE

WEASEL. Hell of a crowd here.
T-BONE. Yellin an carryin signs. Dont like the looks of it.
WEASEL. Lets check it out.
T-BONE. Could be the Klan.
WEASEL. Naw theys black folk too.
T-BONE. Whats that they sayin.
WEASEL. Souns like no nukes, no nukes.
T-BONE. Whats a nuke.
WEASEL. You know. Them little Oriental fellas, come here after the war.
T-BONE. An they gainst them. What I tell you. Ever way you turn another damn biggot.
WEASEL. Man climbin the platform.
DOC TATUM. Friends an noble citizens o the esteemed municipality o Frogmore. For those who dont know me, I be jest a country doctor. A pore doctor whose only fee is the welfare an safety o the residents along Port Royal Sound. So what, you may well ask yourself, is a country doctor doin on top the stump spoutin off like some kinda know-it-all bout nookular power. What am I doin here.
T-BONE. Beats the fuck outa me.
WEASEL. Let him talk T-Bone mebbe you *learn* somethin.
T-BONE. Only thing I wanna know is where folk findin this corn on the cob.
WEASEL. Fine go look fer it I wait here.
DOC TATUM. What are any of us doin here, soakin ourselves with sweat an sea air, tired an hungry. How bout you young man.
WEASEL. Who me.
DOC TATUM. Thass right come on up here where we kin all see you. *(Pause.)* Tell us yer name son. *(Pause.)* Go head we aint gonna bite you.

WEASEL. Weas...William.
DOC TATUM. Where you from Bill.
WEASEL. Greenville.
DOC TATUM. Greenville thass a long journey. What brings you to our fine community.
WEASEL. Lookin fer work.
DOC TATUM. You hear that folks. The man is *looking for work*. Find anythin yet.
WEASEL. Well not exactly -
DOC TATUM. Course not you know why not I tell you why not. *Indifference*. Plain an simple. Who the hell cares bout you.
WEASEL. *(Pause.)* Dunno.
DOC TATUM. I do. I care bout you Billy. An I wanna do my best to find you a job.
WEASEL. How bout somethin in sales.
DOC TATUM. Gotta git elected first Bill. You kin step down now.
WEASEL. Thanks Doc.
DOC TATUM. Now I -
WEASEL. An thanks to the city of Frogmore. Its a pleasure to be passin through sech a nice town.
DOC TATUM. Fine fine git youself some corn while its hot. *(Pause.)* Now I hear you askin, whats wrong with the district representatives we awready got. What makes *you* so different. Well all I got to say is its bout time we had a feller in the Statehouse who knows somethin bout *disease*. I aint jest talkin bout the putrefaction o the flesh. Im talkin bout a disease o the spirit. The kind o disease that leads to nookular waste in your neighborhood. Dont let that disease infect the glorious land o Port Royal Sound. Vote for Doctor Lyle Tatum. Thank you.
T-BONE. He done?
WEASEL. Where you been.
T-BONE. Workin the crowd. Looky here. Two wallets an a bracelet.
WEASEL. You missed somethin lemme tell you. I gotta talk to this feller.

T-BONE. Wha for the man could pop corn in his mouth.
WEASEL. You wrong T-Bone hey Doctor Doctor.
DOC TATUM. Lyle Tatum. Glad to meet you thanks fer comin out showin your support proud citizens like you gonna bring bout brighter days in the tidelands. Will you help us in our noble efforts by takin up one o these plexiglass protest signs.
T-BONE. Whats it pay.
DOC TATUM. Thass a good point my friend but Im sorely afraid all I have to offer is the eternal gratitude o the good common folk o South Carolina.
T-BONE. Hell even the unions pay a dolla a day.
WEASEL. See Doc we aint been eatin too reglar an a little bit o sustinance could go a long way with us. We might could even spread the word long to a whole slew o folk aint got no permanent address. Theys a lotta folk like us be glad to vote fer a feller like you.
DOC TATUM. My friend you have touched my conscience down to its very core. The plight o the homeless is one o the central thrusts o my campaign. Please be my guests at my house tonight for the Virginia end of a ham an cornbread.
T-BONE. A*wright*.
WEASEL. We dont wanna take advantage.
DOC TATUM. Not at all.
T-BONE. Caint say no to a man as hospital as you.
WEASEL. Any nuke shows his face roun here gonna have to deal with *us*.

DOC TATUM'S PORCH

DOC TATUM. You boys git yer fill?
T-BONE. Yessir. That hit the spot all right.
DOC TATUM. Got some news fer you boys.
WEASEL. Whats that.
DOC TATUM. A surprise. You gonna git yer picture took.
T-BONE. By who.
DOC TATUM. City paper. They gonna do a story on you. You boys gonna have jobs fore you know it.
WEASEL. Hear that T-Bone what I tell you bout this feller. How kin we thank you proper.
DOC TATUM. Jest enjoy yourselves.
WEASEL. Thank the man T-Bone what wrong with you.
T-BONE. Dont want my picture took.
WEASEL. Course you do.
T-BONE. Dont want nobody lookin at me.
DOC TATUM. Fine fine we discuss it later have some more Jack Daniel. Now tell me true what you think o the speech.
T-BONE. You done raise the devil all right.
DOC TATUM. But what did you think. I wanna know yer per*spect*ive as a coupla citizens abused an betrayed by society.
T-BONE. That us?
DOC TATUM. The way I see you. How do you see yourself.
T-BONE. A car thief.
DOC TATUM. You are a creature o God.
WEASEL. T-Bone dont believe in God.
T-BONE. God aint got no use fer the likes o me.
DOC TATUM. He looks after each an ever one o his creations.
T-BONE. You ever see a possum git squashed by a semi.
WEASEL. Last piece o pie.
DOC TATUM. Take it I git the phone. *(Pause.)* Tatum. Where you at Skippy tole you to be here eight sharp with photographers. *(Pause.)* Nother assignment you tell me what they got thats better

than Doc Tatum feedin a coupla bums week fore election. They keep askin fer human interest soon as you give em some where the hell are they. Four alarm fire hell gotta be somebody left. *(Pause.)* God no not that cross-eyed fool last time he took my picture I looked like a burn victim. Okay Skippy you done right jest line it up fer tomorrow night I make sure they still be here hold on. *(Pause.)* Hey boys if you not too busy why not stay a coupla days. Free room an board till you feel good an refreshed cant beat that now can you.
T-BONE. Dont know bout this Weasel.
WEASEL. Whats on the menu.
DOC TATUM. Hell I dunno how bout some nice veal hold on whats that Skippy. *(Pause.)* Right veals too ostentatious how bout fried chicken. Good boys how does fried chicken an mashed potatoes sound.
WEASEL. Jest dandy.
DOC TATUM. Right eight o clock tell em I gonna take em in that should git their asses over here. *(Pause.)* Sorry boys a little campaign bizness now where were we.
T-BONE. Talkin bout yer speech.
WEASEL. I liked it.
DOC TATUM. You did now.
WEASEL. Liked it a bunch. Minded me o that feller on the 700 Club.
DOC TATUM. I got plans fer this state boys. Big plans.
WEASEL. Kin tell that jest by lookin at you. Whatcha plannin to do.
DOC TATUM. Lookin fer some Jim Beam. Here it is.
WEASEL. I mean when you git elected. You gonna turn things roun aint ya.
DOC TATUM. You damn right I gonna turn things round. I give you my solemn promise that I aint gonna let up till I wipe out ever pocket o poverty in this district. I tell you how come. As God is my witness I mean what I bout to say from the bottom o my heart. I *hate* poor people. I hate lookin at em an I hate livin near em. I hate the way they look the way they smell an most of all I hate the pathetic

look o dejection an humiliation on their faces. Gives me a headache jest to think bout it. Disturbs my sleep.

WEASEL. I know what you mean.

DOC TATUM. Speakin o which its bout that time. You boys make yourself comfy spare room down the hall bathroom next to it. Tomorrow we give some reporters a call an they can watch me give both o you thorough medical examinations for free. Either o you got hookworms?

WEASEL. No sir.

DOC TATUM. Damn. You sure? Tell you what I check yer stools in the mornin an mebbe we get lucky. Night now.

T-BONE. *(Pause.)* I got his car keys. Lets go.

WEASEL. Put them back T-Bone.

T-BONE. Whats wrong with you.

WEASEL. Not him. This is different.

T-BONE. What is.

WEASEL. He cares bout us. Wants to hep us.

T-BONE. He *gonna* hep us. That Chrysler gonna hep us get to Florida. Time he shakes off that Jim Beam we be in Key West.

WEASEL. Aint gonna do it T-Bone.

T-BONE. Dont be a fool Weasel we be *nothin* to this man talkin bout us like some kind o damn *animal*. Settin right there in front of us sayin how bad we stink.

WEASEL. He dont mean us.

T-BONE. He mean ever one but *him*.

WEASEL. Dammit T-Bone we gettin fed at last an you wanna fuck it up.

T-BONE. You jest hearin what you wanna hear.

WEASEL. I gettin sick o you T-Bone so proud o sayin how nothin matters, given up fore you even try.

T-BONE. Thass right. Comin or aint you.

WEASEL. Not with you.

T-BONE. You rather kiss ass all yer life.

WEASEL. An you rather be an empty sack. A *loser*. *(Pause.)* Ahhhhhhhhhhhhhh.

T-BONE. *(Long pause.)* You hurt me Weasel. Why you wanna hurt me.
WEASEL. Look at this blood. Shit.
T-BONE. I break yer nose?
WEASEL. Probly.
T-BONE. You shouldna said that.
WEASEL. Git out.
T-BONE. Yeah. *(Pause.)* See you.

IN THE DARK

WEASEL. Doc Tatum? *(Pause.)* Doc. Doc Tatum. Wake up.
DOC TATUM. That you Skippy.
WEASEL. No sir. Its me. Weasel. You took us in, member? Fed us some ham.
DOC TATUM. What the hell you want. Dont you try nothin I got a gun right here.
WEASEL. No no it aint nothin like that. Look kin I turn on the light. Its somethin important.
DOC TATUM. *(Pause.)* Go head. *(Pause.)* You woke me up cause of a nosebleed.
WEASEL. No sir.
DOC TATUM. Tilt yer head back an put ice on it. Good night.
WEASEL. Its bout T-Bone. He borrowed yer car.
DOC TATUM. *(Pause.)* Borrowed it.
WEASEL. Cept he might fergit to bring it back.
DOC TATUM. Lemme git this straight. He attacked you an stole my car.
WEASEL. He didnt attack me.
DOC TATUM. He didnt.
WEASEL. Naw. He jest...hit me.
DOC TATUM. I see.
WEASEL. I said somethin stupid. I deserved it. This is all my fault.
DOC TATUM. Hand me that phone.
WEASEL. He dont even know where he be goin. He jest headin fer more trouble.
DOC TATUM. Thass fer sure.
WEASEL. I cant let him do that to hisself. Know what Im sayin Doc Im worried about him.
DOC TATUM. You did the right thing son. We gonna bring him back here dont you fret.
WEASEL. He aint a bad man Doc. He jest needs a little...what you call it..

DOC TATUM. Rehabilitatin.
WEASEL. Yeah thass it. You gonna help him aint ya? Dont send him back to Black River.
DOC TATUM. I wont press charges. You have my word.

A PRISON CELL

T-BONE. Hunh? Who there.
BROTHER TIM. Just me.
T-BONE. A preacher. Dont want no preacher.
BROTHER TIM. Brother Tim.
T-BONE. Dont care if you Father Time git outa my cell.
BROTHER TIM. Wanna cigarette?
T-BONE. No I dont wanna cigarette I wanna know why you preachers gotta assume ever body lyin in a jail cell caint wait to feast they eyes on a man o the cloth. This gonna be hard fer you to unnerstan but I dont want you. I want a woman. Git me a woman or ask God to send me one. While you at it tell him I want a few answers to some questions disturbin my mind. Sech as if God be so disgusted with the human race that he set up places like this why dint he jest wipe us all out with the Flood in the first place. Or is it all some kinda *game* with him like the one he played with Abraham. Some angel come down an tell me to sacrifice *my* son I whip that angels ass. An Job what a sorry son of a bitch standin roun thankin God ever time he gits kicked in the nuts. I wont put up with that shit an you can go tell that to God. And where the hell did Jesus go, up there watchin the dog races ever day whens he plannin to come back anyway. Mebbe he jest plain *forgot.* An whats God got to offer a feller like me? He gonna stick me in some place where all I do is sit aroun worshippin *him?* Got news fer you Brother Tim that might be *yore* idea of eternal bliss but it jest dont cut it with me. Tell you somethin else. I seen them pictures o God when I was in school and the cat is *white.* So what you got to say Brother Tim I be all ears lay the Word on me.
BROTHER TIM. *(Pause.)* Wanna cigarette?

CLAYBORNE CONSTRUCTION COMPANY

WEASEL. Howdy do sir. William Weasler at yer service. I heard bout yer ad an jest wanted to quire bout the bricklayin job.
CLAYBORNE. I. Knnnow. You.
WEASEL. Lawd in heaven you the man back in that church basement.
CLAYBORNE. You. Gave. Mmmme.
WEASEL. A tellygram right well theys a proper explanation fer that see Western Union done mixed up the wires. Course I took the blame an fore you know it I be outa the messenger service you dont believe a word o this do you.
CLAYBORNE. Nnnno.
WEASEL. I be on my way now.
CLAYBORNE. Hold. On. You. Got. The. Job.
WEASEL. I do?
CLAYBORNE. I. Won. The swee. The swee.
WEASEL. The sweepstakes? You won the sweepstakes?
CLAYBORNE. Nnnnow. Immmm. Rich.
WEASEL. I had it in my hands. In my very hands. An now you work here. Wait a minute. Clayborne Construction. You own it.
CLAYBORNE. Mmme. And. Nnnna. Than.

THE PRISON CELL

T-BONE. Hunh what now who are you.
REVEREND GLUCK. The Lawd Awmighty bless you an preserve you now an forever.
T-BONE. Reverend Gluck.
REVEREND GLUCK. Kind sir you member the man I was only pretendin to be. But alas it was only a disguise to cover a multitude o sins. I stand afore you one William Weasler, former resident o Greenville, now yer cellmate for the heenous crime o patricide.
T-BONE. What you sayin. They took you in fer killin Weasels daddy?
REVEREND GLUCK. I give up peaceful. They have all the evidence they need. The murder weapon. Identification. Fingerprints. Motive.
T-BONE. What motive?
REVEREND GLUCK. I hated my daddy.
T-BONE. But he aint yer daddy. They got the wrong man.
REVEREND GLUCK. Beg to differ son. I confessed to the murder.
T-BONE. *(Pause.)* You total crazy now aint you.
REVEREND GLUCK. Crazy...is a Willie Nelson song. I like Willie Nelson. You like Willie Nelson?
T-BONE. Listen Reverend you aint William Weasler. You jest think you are.
REVEREND GLUCK. Thass where you wrong. I think Im Reverend Gluck. Thank heaven the authorities found me in time. They gonna send me to a place where they got drugs to help me member.
T-BONE. You dint kill him.
REVEREND GLUCK. You jest said I was crazy.
T-BONE. You are. But William Weasler is my friend.
REVEREND GLUCK. Thank you son. You my friend too. I jest pray I dont strangle you in yer sleep.

WEASEL'S BEDROOM

T-BONE. Weeeeasel. Wake up Weasel.
WEASEL. Go way T-Bone. You still in prison.
T-BONE. We got some bizness Weasel.
WEASEL. You aint even real. You jest a nightmare.
T-BONE. You been havin this nightmare a lot.
WEASEL. Look what do you want.
T-BONE. To beat the stuffin outa you.
WEASEL. Dammit T-Bone git outa here I gotta be up at six.
T-BONE. They lettin me out next month. Aint you fraid I gonna be lookin fer you?
WEASEL. Course I aint afraid. I gonna drive to Black River to pick you up.
T-BONE. Who gonna pick *you* up?
WEASEL. Where the hell are you.
T-BONE. In yer pillowcase. You been sleepin on my face.
WEASEL. You caint scare me.
T-BONE. What say I twist yer head off an use it fer a basketball.
WEASEL. Stay way from me T-Bone I mean it owww leggo leggo my head no dont tear it off you pullin me outa bed stop it shit. *(Pause.)* Where you at now.
T-BONE. Still in yer pillow. Night Weasel.
WEASEL. Look I doin fine without you. Got my own place, food on the table, gonna buy a *car* what you think o that T-Bone a car you dint even *steal*. When you git out I gonna hep you git back on yer feet then I kin sleep again.
T-BONE. Think so.
WEASEL. Thass right now I gonna go back to sleep an I dont care if you in my pillow or not.
T-BONE. *(Pause.)* You need a shave.

THE GATES OF BLACK RIVER PENITENTIARY

WEASEL. I swear T-Bone its damn good to see you again. What say we put this place behind you.
T-BONE. Still dont know how they found me on the road to Florida.
WEASEL. Best not to think bout it no more.
T-BONE. Where you learn to drive.
WEASEL. Triple A Drivin School.
T-BONE. Git yer money back.
WEASEL. Like my car?
T-BONE. Its a *Chevette*.
WEASEL. Thass right you got somethin gainst compacts.
T-BONE. Jest Chevettes. You git that piece I ask for?
WEASEL. Why you need somethin like that T-Bone you jest got *out* for Chrissakes.
T-BONE. Where is it.
WEASEL. Aint got the need fer one now I got a job all lined up for you in Columbia.
T-BONE. The *piece* Weasel.
WEASEL. Under the seat. *(Pause.)*
T-BONE. This it?
WEASEL. Course what you think.
T-BONE. Kin barely *see* this thing. I got fingers bigger than this barrel.
WEASEL. Its a snubnose.
T-BONE. Its a piece o shit.
WEASEL. Look I lost my ole contacts I did what I could.
T-BONE. Good thing I dont have a hole in my pocket.
WEASEL. Guess you heard Doc Tatum won the election. *(Pause.)* Oww leggo leggo I tryin to drive.
T-BONE. Two things I dont wanna hear agin. One is the name o Doc Tatum. The other is the word "Loser."
WEASEL. Got you.

T-BONE. Good. Now git off the highway take the county road.
WEASEL. Where we goin.
T-BONE. Gonna pay somebody a visit.
WEASEL. Look I went to a lotta trouble to git you this job.
T-BONE. Sorry Weasel we gonna take a little detour. Got a score to settle.

HAPPY SAM'S USED CARS

WEASEL. Place all boarded up T-Bone. Lets go.
T-BONE. I dint come all this way fer nothin. He gotta be here.
WEASEL. Anybody there!
HAPPY SAM. Go to hell!
T-BONE. Thass him.
HAPPY SAM. I be tryin to sleep here. We aint open. Aint buyin aint sellin.
T-BONE. Aint leavin till we see you.
HAPPY SAM. Whos we.
WEASEL. T-Bone and Weasel.
HAPPY SAM. This look like a butcher shop boy now hit the highway.
T-BONE. Aint sellin meat.
HAPPY SAM. Had weasel once dont even make good stew.
WEASEL. Look T-Bone what you got in mind here anyhow.
T-BONE. Open up or we force the door.
HAPPY SAM. *(Pause.)* There you happy now what the hell you want.
T-BONE. Wanna talk to you.
HAPPY SAM. Bout what.
T-BONE. Dont you member me.
HAPPY SAM. What is this shit now you gonna make me *guess*.
T-BONE. We done bizness with you bout a year ago.
HAPPY SAM. That narrows it down dont it.
T-BONE. You bought a Buick from me fer a hunnerd five dollas.
HAPPY SAM. No kiddin musta circled that day on my calendar.
T-BONE. Mebbe this hep you member.
HAPPY SAM. What the hell you call that dont even look like a real gun.
T-BONE. Try me.

63

WEASEL. Now you done it we gonna go right back to prison.
HAPPY SAM. Now I suppose you gonna kill me.
T-BONE. Thinkin bout it.
HAPPY SAM. Thinkin bout it you mean you dont even *know*. I supposed to stand aroun in my shorts while you make up yer mind.
T-BONE. Shut up.
HAPPY SAM. Oh I know its the *suspense* of it aint it. You want me to stand here shakin while I wonder what you gonna do to me.
T-BONE. Aint afraid o nothin are you.
HAPPY SAM. Hell I had so many guns an knives stuck in my face I lost count. Folk try to poison my food. Hit me with their cars. Somebody put a cottonmouth in my mailbox jest last week. Hell my own dog tried to kill me till I had him shot.
WEASEL. Mebbe its yer attitude.
HAPPY SAM. Who asked you dickface. Now shoot me or git out.
T-BONE. We want our money back. Five thousand.
HAPPY SAM. Fine jest take yer pop gun to the county attorney an rob *him*. He took everthin I own cept my teeth.
T-BONE. You sayin the law shut you down.
HAPPY SAM. Cuzed me o sellin stolen property. Course now *they* git to sell it dont they.
WEASEL. We wastin time here T-Bone.
HAPPY SAM. So long boys. *(Pause.)* What the hell is that a *Chevette*.
T-BONE. *(Long pause.)* Awright Weasel lets check out this job o yours.
WEASEL. You wont be sorry T-Bone jest wait till you feel that steady paycheck in yer pocket. Whole new life fer you earnin some *respeck* fer yourself.
T-BONE. Now dont *push* me. I say I try it. Thass all.

FUTURE HOME OF COLUMBIA TRUST

T-BONE. What first.
WEASEL. See that stack o tile.
T-BONE. Yep.
WEASEL. Start in the corner an lay it out.
T-BONE. Okay. What then.
WEASEL. Do the next room.
T-BONE. No I mean what else I git to do.
WEASEL. You aint even started this job an now you want another one.
T-BONE. Aint sayin that.
WEASEL. Then what you want.
T-BONE. Jest dont wanna do the same thing all day. I like a little variety.
WEASEL. I tole them this be your *specialty* T-Bone. Once you git a specialty you gotta stick with it. I do bricks. You do tile.
T-BONE. An thass all I do. Forever an ever.
WEASEL. Thass right. You a free man now. Take advantage of it.
T-BONE. Shit.
WEASEL. Now git started an I check back on you.
T-BONE. Hey Weasel.
WEASEL. What now.
T-BONE. Somebody sleepin here behind the tile.
WEASEL. Hell not again wake up you.
T-BONE. Hey dont you scarin him.
WEASEL. Thass the point.
T-BONE. Aint wearin nothin but a raincoat. Who is he.
WEASEL. Some derelict thinks he got the right to spend the night here. Cant tell you how many times I have to kick him out.
T-BONE. I dont see him hurtin nobody.
WEASEL. He aint right in the head. Look at him throwin his arms

around.

T-BONE. Look like a dog been beat too much.

WEASEL. He gotta go fore they find him here an we git in trouble.

T-BONE. Mans got some demons to fight. Who you swingin at feller. I be able to hep you if you tell me who to ketch.

WEASEL. Dont *talk* to him T-Bone you jest encouragin him.

T-BONE. What wrong with that. Gimme a sandwich.

WEASEL. No way Jose this gotta git me through the day.

T-BONE. You got two sandwiches there.

WEASEL. I *work* T-Bone. I *burn* this food.

T-BONE. I say give it here. *(Pause.)* Here you go feller. Like some tuna salad. *(Pause.)* Nice raincoat. Too bad you got paint on it.

RAINCOAT. Blood.

T-BONE. *(Pause.)* Wanna bite?

RAINCOAT. *(Pause.)* I guess.

WEASEL. Jesus T-Bone now we never git rid of him.

T-BONE. You got a name feller.

RAINCOAT. Nope.

T-BONE. Me neither. How bout I call you Raincoat.

RAINCOAT. I guess.

WEASEL. Look its my ass on the line you know. I *got* you this job I be responsible fer you.

T-BONE. Well I be relievin you o that Weasel.

WEASEL. Guess you want us both out on the street again that what you want.

T-BONE. Keep this shit up I gonna quit.

WEASEL. Now aint that smart. Go head run away like you did with Doc Tatums car. See if I bring you back this time.

T-BONE. *(Pause.)* What you mean bring me back.

WEASEL. I always lookin out fer you T-Bone keepin you outa trouble. I woke up Doc Tatum tole him you stole his car.

T-BONE. You set me up fer Black River.

WEASEL. Now that aint my fault. Tatum said he wouldn press charges.

T-BONE. An you believed that.
WEASEL. Hell I gotta believe in *somethin* dont I.
T-BONE. *(Pause.)* Someone callin yer name.
WEASEL. Shit thass the foreman I be in fer it now. Make sure you git him outa here I be right back.
T-BONE. *(Pause.)* Dont mind him jest rest yer legs awhile. Taste good dont it.
RAINCOAT. I guess.
T-BONE. Used to git in a lot o fights myself. In the State Reformatory. Thirteen years old. You ever there.
RAINCOAT. Nope.
T-BONE. You lucky. *(Pause.)* Ran away once. They sent some dogs out an caught me. Took me back to this big room with a mattress on the floor. Had to lie face down while they hit me with a strap. Had little holes cut in the leather so it would tear strips o skin off. An if I cried they start all over. But I dint cry. I jest lay there. An took it. *(Pause.)* Few days later I took a knife in the shin.
WEASEL. You tole me it was a rat terrier.
T-BONE. I know. *(Pause.)* You feel like gettin up now Raincoat? Cause I gotta git at this tile soon. I be a company man now.
WEASEL. No you aint. Foreman jest let you go.
T-BONE. How come.
WEASEL. He say I never tole him you was colored.
T-BONE. Fergot that little fact now did you.
WEASEL. Like I tole you before T-Bone I dont think bout them things.
T-BONE. Now you see where that gits you.
WEASEL. *(Pause.)* What you gonna do now.
T-BONE. I be hittin the highway.
WEASEL. Where you goin.
T-BONE. What you care.
WEASEL. You off to git youself arrested agin aint you.
T-BONE. Mebbe.
WEASEL. Or killed.
T-BONE. Look you got somethin to say then say it.
WEASEL. Lemme come with you.

T-BONE. *(Pause.)* You expeck me to take you along. Somebody I thought was my *friend*.
WEASEL. I am yer friend.
T-BONE. You sent me to *prison*.
WEASEL. I aint always a *good* friend.
T-BONE. *(Pause.)* You got a good thing goin here Weasel.
WEASEL. They fired you T-Bone.
T-BONE. That dont bother me.
WEASEL. It bothers me.
T-BONE. *(Pause.)* Could be dangerous.
WEASEL. Okay by me.
T-BONE. I dunno Weasel.
WEASEL. You kin hit me if you want.
T-BONE. Dont wanna hit you.
WEASEL. Shore you do go head you know it make you feel better. Grab me twist my arm.
T-BONE. Dont have to do that.
WEASEL. How come.
T-BONE. I git *him* to do it. Hey Raincoat. He all yours.

ANOTHER HIGHWAY

WEASEL. I tell you we be headin fer trouble T-Bone.
T-BONE. Hey Raincoat. Do we git yer word you aint gonna rob or kill us tween here an the state line?
RAINCOAT. I guess.
T-BONE. There you go, Weasel.
WEASEL. That good nuff fer you?
T-BONE. The most we kin ask for.
RAINCOAT. Im hungry.
WEASEL. *Live* with it. Look T-Bone I still wanna be prepared.
T-BONE. Okay I got a pen out. Dont take all night.
WEASEL. This be the last will an testament o William Weasler, formerly of Greenville, South Carolina. Bein o sound mind -
T-BONE. That be the day.
WEASEL. You mind yourself. This a sacred document.
T-BONE. What the hell you gonna leave anybody.
WEASEL. In the event o my death, I would like my Mama to have all the money left over at the moment o my departure.
T-BONE. Anythin else.
WEASEL. To my best an only friend T-Bone -
T-BONE. Shit Weasel -
WEASEL. Take it *down*. To T-Bone I leave my most prized possession - my car.
T-BONE. You gonna give me a goddamn Chevette an thirty-two car payments?
WEASEL. You dont want it.
T-BONE. Hell no I dont want it.
WEASEL. How bout a tape containin Creedence Clearwater greatest hits.
T-BONE. *No.*
WEASEL. How bout you Raincoat you like CCR.
RAINCOAT. Proud Mary.
WEASEL. Thass the one.
RAINCOAT. Green River.

WEASEL. Yep.
RAINCOAT. Keep on Chooglin.
WEASEL. Hear this T-Bone.
RAINCOAT. Ramble Tamble.
WEASEL. Damn right.
RAINCOAT. Ooby Dooby.
WEASEL. Thass right thass right you like em *too* doncha.
RAINCOAT. Nope.
T-BONE. *(Pause.)* You done.
WEASEL. Now your turn.
T-BONE. Come off it Weasel.
WEASEL. You be surprised. It give you some piece of mind.
T-BONE. For Chrissake. This here be the last will an testament o T-Bone.
WEASEL. Gotta use yer real name.
T-BONE. I dont have a damn thing an I never did. But if I do happen to own anythin at the time o my death...nobody gits to have it. Signed an witnessed, Thomas J Bone. *(Pause.)* You right Weasel. I feel a whole lot better.
WEASEL. Which way T-Bone. We got four directions.
RAINCOAT. Head south.